The Delicate Science of Making Love

Disclaimer

Author's Notes

The dialogues and stories in this book are based on the conversations I've had during the years of helping, counseling, studying, and interviewing couples. In order to preserve the privacy of the people involved, names and other identifiable aspects have been changed.

I also want to take the time to show my gratitude to everyone who has let me observe and learn from their relationships over the years—both the struggling and the happy couples. Without all of you, I wouldn't be able to help so many others.

He and She

Even though, at the time of this writing, my other books are mainly aimed at women and written about men, this book knows no gender. I will intertwine she and he because the message will be important to both parties. It takes a team to make a relationship work, and true love can only exist when both sides truly understand each other.

What You're About to Learn

I Do

"I was thinking of you earlier," Sarah says as I kiss her on the cheeks. She looks absolutely stellar; her blond hair is put up in a sophisticated twist, and she is wearing a white lace dress with white heels. She's a ravishing bride.

"Really? You were thinking of me?" I ask, a bit surprised. It is a strange statement, especially that day.

She affirms with a soft voice, "Yes. I've been thinking about everything we discussed a couple of days ago, and I wasn't sure what my answer would be. I still have my doubts...."

"But you said yes," I reply, trying to hide my bewilderment as well as I could.

"I just really hope it's the right decision," Sarah adds.

"I hope so too," I answer, smiling as authentically as possible while slowly walking away.

What a weird experience. *I hope he didn't overhear us*, I tell myself. *He was standing right next to her. And sure, he was caught up in a conversation with other people, but still... if he did overhear, he's going to want to know what she was talking about. He's her husband now, after all.*

Twenty minutes later, I am walking around a large room filled with nicely dressed people and search for my nametag on one of the many decorated tables. I carefully pin the nametag to my lapel and move to my assigned table. An elderly woman looks up and smiles with her overly red lips as I sit down beside her. "Isn't this the most amazing wedding you've ever been to?" she asks.

"It sure is," I say with a fake grin on my face. "One of a kind."

"Sarah and John are such a lucky couple," the woman adds.

I beg to differ but decide it would be unwise to share that insight. I always thought those who said "I do" didn't have such doubts, especially on their big day. And Sarah's uncertainties must have been sizeable, considering she openly communicated them to a guest, only minutes after their bond had been eternalized—as in forever—with her new husband standing beside her. But Sarah had her reasons to be fearful.

***

"There she is," I yell as I drive up to Sarah's place on a beautiful fall evening. I pull over, push open the car door, and tell her to get in. We're about to get drinks and catch up. It's been six months since her wedding, and I haven't seen her for a while.

"So, how have you been?" I ask as I start driving again.

No answer.

I look over, and Sarah is staring at me, trying to communicate a message she can't put into words yet.

"Where's your wedding ring?" I notice out loud.

"It's gone. We're filing for divorce," Sarah replies with tears in her eyes. "It's over. It's all over...." The first tears start to make their way down her face. I immediately realize it is going to be an emotional evening. And it was. A bit like seeing *The*

Notebook, *Titanic*, and *Bambi* on the same night but much worse.

***

A couple of months after that poignant night, I was helping her move out of the shiny penthouse she and her hubby had been utterly miserable in. To be honest, their problems had started long before they got married. That's what she had confessed to me a couple of days prior to the wedding. She was a friend, and I was devastated. I also felt guilty; I had been studying successful relationships for a while and was occasionally coaching people with a variety of emotional challenges—from anxiety and panic attacks to relationship issues. I wished she had come to me earlier. We might have been able to revive and save her relationship, but now we'd never know.

That was the defining moment for me, well over a decade ago. The moment I decided to leave my successful corporate career, put my master's degree in economic sciences in a box in the attic, and start studying a different form of science: the science of why we do what we do. I wanted to start making a difference in people's lives, full time.

Sometimes things are not meant to be, and there are problems we face that we have absolutely no control over. My mission is to help people with the problems and challenges we *can* control. Love, in many cases, is one of them.

What had happened here? Why did she say "I do" when she had her doubts? Why did he? She and her now ex-husband seemed so in love and yet that had all dissipated. Why is love so elusive? Why can it be there one day and gone the next? Why does everything change for some people as soon as they move in together, get married, or have children? Why do people who seem so right for each other fall out of love without warning? Or *is* there a warning? Is there a science, an art behind all of this? How do couples that stay madly in love for decades, truly until death does part them, do it?

Figuring this out has been my mission ever since I was a young boy, given that my parents had a very unstable relationship with more yelling than your average death metal concert. Nevertheless, I didn't want to decipher love just for me but for everyone who wants to make something great of their relationship. For anyone who finds themselves on the brink of the end of a relationship. For people who are struggling in a marriage or a relationship that simply isn't what it used to be. For everyone who wants to feel genuinely loved by their partner.

It turns out those who make love work *have* a secret. Many secrets, in fact. They have a set of very specific habits that keep pumping life and love into the relationship.

They know the delicate science of *making* love.

I have been coaching people with relationship and marital troubles for a very long time now, and whenever I explain what you're about to read to people who were in trouble in their relationship, it has given them clarity. I will share some of their stories with you as well.

Many books have been written about love, and some of them are really good. I am certainly not reinventing the wheel here, but I was always missing the bigger picture—an easy roadmap so to speak. After all, when you're lost in a maze, only a map can get you out and set you back on course. I can't wait to share that map with you.

Why Relationships Get in Trouble

When you ask anyone for advice about love and relationships, even when you go to some experienced relationship therapists, you'll often hear that the secret to lasting love is *communication*.

These well-meaning people are not pulling that concept out of thin air. When I started to interview successful couples to find out their secrets, the great majority told me right off the bat: "Relationships require hard work, and communication is really important." Surely, communication must be it then.

Yet, we all know couples that communicate with the accuracy of a Swiss watch whose relationship is about as passionate as a painting of a stop sign.

When I dug deeper during my interviews of successful couples to get to the *real* answers, it became very apparent that the true secret is very simple: *both partners made sure the other one never felt unloved.*

That was it. It's the big "secret."

And when they made a mistake—given that they are human—and hurt their partner or harmed the precious bond between them, fixing it and making their partner feel loved again became the top priority.

Couples that are not on this mission seem to fail more often than not. That's one of the many reasons why I advocate to not play any games in a relationship. Even if game playing would lead to a change in behavior from our lover, the "love" or attention we'd get wouldn't feel genuine; we would still feel unloved. There's a better and much more satisfying approach.

Communication is not the Holy Grail. It can even hurt a relationship when it's done improperly. If my girlfriend and I fight a lot and I try to explain to her that I'm hurt and how it's all her fault—how she lets me down time and time again, makes mistakes, and is not living up to my standards (thus, depicting myself as the evangelical saint who plays absolutely no role in any of it)—I *am* communicating my feelings. However, she will undoubtedly feel unloved in the process, given that she's now in a courtroom where everything she says and does can and clearly will be used against her, perpetually. It's always a lot easier to see and communicate what the other one is doing wrong than to realize how we might have also played a role in what happened.

The woman who shouts: "Why don't you ever clean up the kitchen when you're done? I feel like a slave in this household! You never remember anything I ask!" *is* communicating and sharing her feelings. Nevertheless, we can both imagine how pleasant the atmosphere will be in her relationship and how high the chances of her boyfriend helping out *more* are. She might as well have yelled: "Do you know the difference between Big Foot and an intelligent man? Big Foot has been spotted several times!" Communicating isn't it. There's a lot more to maintaining a lasting, loving relationship.

When both parties' top priority is to make the other person feel loved, lasting love gets the room and fertilizer it desperately needs to grow.
If you're reading this book because you've become unhappy in your relationship, I'm willing to bet it's because your partner is making you feel unloved. Feeling unloved is the root cause of many relationship issues.

Relationships get in trouble when either party feels unloved and the other party doesn't do what's required to fix it. When, for any reason, either of the parties starts to see the other one as the enemy or as the cause of feeling hurt, the fuse has been lit. Explosions, deafening silence, or withdrawal will follow.

On the other hand, when both parties see the relationship as a fortress they need to vigorously protect, the fairy tale can begin and happily ever after has a shot of playing out.

You may wonder how we can make sure both parties feel loved. In my experience, it's based on a comprehensive understanding of what both lovers need to feel loved, combined with lavishly using emotional intelligence (side-stepping a lot of the unwarranted emotions and thoughts our ego will serve us). When either party becomes selfish, the fortress is in danger.

We don't *just* need to communicate within relationships; we need to do so in such a way that makes our lover feel loved and never *un*loved. However, as we will see time and time again in this book, what makes one person feel loved, may not move the meter an inch on another person. We are all wired differently. That's where the concept of the love ponds comes in.

The Seven Love Ponds

Love yourself. That's the advice you get from everyone. It's spot on. We should indeed never place our happiness in the hands of another person, and we should always remain at the reins of our own wellbeing. That makes sense. However, we can have an incredibly healthy amount of self-love, but when we're in a relationship with someone who ignores us or doesn't seem to love us any longer, very powerful and primitive alarms are triggered. All the self-love in the world isn't able to save us from the negative feelings and anxiety that take over whenever we feel like we're losing our relationship.

After my newly wedded friend got divorced, I went through the scientific research on love and examined results from previous clients. I also gained powerful insights from my coaching challenges, considering some couples still didn't make it. I, sadly, was not a love guru with magical powers. That motivated me even more; I needed to figure this out.

At that time, I was still missing something. When I looked at the couples I had personally been in touch with, I wondered what was different for those that made it. I also reviewed my own failed relationships. After reviewing my interviews with (at that time) hundreds of successful couples, the truth finally hit me with the weight of someone who just drove 13 hours in the wrong direction: love, in long-term relationships, doesn't just *exist* between two people. It's not something that magically appears. We cannot leave it to chance or Cupid. It needs to be *created and maintained*. To do so, we must pay close attention to what I'll call our unique set of love ponds, which we'll dive into a detailed explanation.

When I started explaining this concept to some of the people I was helping, magic happened. Finally! At first, I couldn't believe it, given that the concept is not really that complex. I thought other factors had to be playing a role. So I explained it to even more people, and to my astonishment, the magic continued. As far as I was concerned, the love ponds were the answer. They were what I had been missing! The difference in behavior was often night and day. Men who had become complacent, who took their girlfriends or wives for granted or worse, ignored them, started to behave like Cupid-stricken teenagers again and couldn't get enough of their girl. Women who had lost respect for their man started to see him as their knight in shining armor once more. Why? Because their love ponds were filled. Going from full to empty and vice-versa can create extreme changes in behavior.

To have a happy relationship, we need to be well aware of what makes both ourselves and our partner feel deeply loved. Everyone is wired differently, and our needs to feel *genuinely* loved are quite diverse. What feels like being loved to you may be different from what your partner feels. And if unmet needs keep stacking up, we start to feel unloved. We also need to steer clear of everything that feels like we're unloved as much as we realistically can. The anthropologist and scientist Helen Fisher calls this concept the hierarchy of needs. Some needs absolutely have to be filled if we want to feel stable and happy. What those needs are will vary for everyone.

Love Ponds Defined

Imagine a magical place with seven pools of water. These ponds each have a waterfall filling them up with fresh water representing love. There are also little streams flowing out of the ponds that empty them. The ponds and streams differ in size, meaning some love ponds empty faster than others.

Some ponds need a *constant* steady stream of love water; otherwise, they will dry out quickly. Other love ponds can sit there for weeks with the water level going down just a bit. In other words, some ponds need a lot more care and attention than others. When your love ponds are filled, you feel great. Absolutely stellar! When your lover's ponds are taken care of, you'll feel warm and genuine affection coming your way.

The size of these ponds is different for all of us and so is the importance of each. Some of your ponds can stay filled for weeks without any additional love flowing into them. You won't feel something is missing if your partner doesn't give them a lot of attention. Others, your more important ponds, need constant care. They empty quickly. And when the water gets to a critical level, you'll feel unloved, possibly needy, and your anxiety and frustration will rise. You won't feel and behave like yourself anymore. Worries arrive, and you'll feel unsafe in the relationship that used to bring you joy. Whereas the relationship may have brought out the best in you before, now the scale is tipping. Important needs that make you feel loved remain unmet. This is when needy behavior, nagging, and maybe even some anger or resentment start to appear. At this point, it feels like your partner is hurting or possibly even using you, and you'll feel like you're being treated unfairly.

We cannot sufficiently fill up the ponds ourselves. The love that fills them mostly has to come from others. It can come from friends and family, but there's nothing that will fill them up faster than loving actions from that special person we love. That's when the true magic happens. Ideally, our romantic partner should find out what matters most to us, what we need to feel loved, to feel safe... and then give it so we can rest assured that our needs are met and will continue to be so. We, on the other hand, should do the same for them. Manipulation, game-playing, nagging, or threatening to leave should never ever be required to feel loved. When you're in a great relationship and your romantic needs are *un*met, when you're in any form of pain, your lover will drop everything and will come to your rescue to fix it. And vice-versa. Relationships are not meant to be any other way.

When your and your partner's love ponds are filled, you'll feel calm, stable, and safe within your relationship. Chances are you'll even be a bundle of joy on most days. At the very least, you'll feel like you can take on the world much more easily. From that stability and that feeling of safety, you can reach higher and higher in the real world and face your daily challenges with excellence.

The Challenge of the Love Ponds

Even though the concept is easy to grasp, the love ponds do come with their own set of challenges. What is loving and important to you may not be important to your partner. Since you love your partner, you could decide to *do* something to make your partner feel loved. Nevertheless, the pond in which you are pouring your love water may not matter that much to your companion. There you are investing in the relationship, trying to show you love your partner, but your lover doesn't seem to feel or acknowledge it; there's no response. It may even have the *opposite* effect. You'll see this play out in plenty of the upcoming examples.

Likewise, if your partner is not filling up your more important love ponds, you'll feel like the one you love doesn't "get" you, ignores what's important to you, and isn't investing nearly as much into the relationship as you are. If his misunderstanding of your ponds is causing him to fill up the wrong ones, you'll feel unloved, empty, and unsatisfied in the relationship while *he* believes he's doing a great job and is treating you like a

17

queen. Or she may be giving it all she's got, but it's seemingly never good enough, which will be very frustrating to her. The relationship will start to feel like a game you just cannot win no matter how hard you try. One step forward, sixteen steps backward. And all of this happens because of a misunderstanding of each other's love ponds and the underlying needs.

On top of that, the order of importance of one's love ponds can *and probably will* vary throughout life. You have surely felt your own needs vary and changing over the years. We need to keep paying attention and be on top of it. There is no autopilot in the game of love.

So what's the solution? Understanding the size and layout of not only our own but our partner's love ponds and making sure that we are not afraid to communicate clearly about what we need to feel loved. What are the sensitive and important ponds to you and your partner? What ponds need a refill? What behaviors make you or your partner feel loved and unloved? The answers to these questions need to be *absolutely* clear.

Once the love status, layouts, and sensitivities of the ponds are found, the next step is making sure that, as a team, we fill them up fully. On top of that, we must pay attention to the major relationship killers like negativity, neediness, nagging, criticism, and resentment. The couples where both partners pay attention to these aspects last for as long as they want. You'll find proof of this concept in the couples you know that seem to effortlessly remain in love decade after decade. You'll understand exactly how they do it by the end of this book. In short, they are masters in the delicate science of making love.

The people who make love last have a deep appreciation for what makes themselves *and* their partners feel fully loved. It's indispensable. They know how to give love and at the same time stand up for what's important to them *in a loving way.* The only way to have love truly flourish is to give genuine love in meaningful ways *without* becoming a doormat or losing our integrity in the process.

And good news! As soon as you start filling up your partner's love ponds, you'll get distinctively more pleasant behavior in return. Your partner will start behaving favorably toward you and your love ponds, especially if you take the time to explain this system. We'll go over each of the seven love ponds and how to fill them later in this book.

From Falling to Failing in Love

"I just don't get it," a desperate Rachel told me with tears in her eyes. "He changed. When we started dating and even when we decided to move in together, I was one of his top priorities. He always made time for me. He listened to me when I came home and wanted to talk about my day. We had fun; we were a couple. But now all he seems to do is work long hours and by the time he gets home, he's a walking zombie that I can't have a normal conversation with. I feel like I have a better bond with our hamster than with Brad."

Rachel had tried to explain to her boyfriend that she wasn't happy with the way things were going. In return, Brad always rolled his eyes and said something to the tune of, "I'm working hard for us. I'm trying to take care of us. Why are you complaining? Can't you see I'm doing this for us, for you?" To which Rachel often replied, "I'd rather live in a small studio with more time to spend together than have a big house while feeling so alone."

Eye-rolling champion Brad thought she was overreacting. He honestly believed he was a victim here. That was a big mistake. As this situation continued, the wedge between them became bigger and bigger. Rachel believed Brad was just making excuses to come home later, to meet friends over the weekend, to spend even *less* time with her. Needless to say, she was heartbroken. But she was also absolutely right.

When I finally got a chance to talk to Brad—who would've rather alphabetically organized his sock drawer than discuss this issue with me—he assured me that he still loved Rachel. "It doesn't seem to matter what I do for her, she doesn't want to acknowledge it. And lately, all she does is complain. She's not really helping out at home either. I'm out there working hard on my career for us, so we can have a good life and don't have to worry about money. I'm trying to build something for both of us. But it seems like she's starting to sabotage it, like she doesn't support me. I'm all alone out there on the battlefield. I admit that this is changing how I feel about Rachel. I don't like to come home anymore; it's no longer my safe place because I know she will complain. I will be criticized, I will need to defend myself, and I just don't have the energy anymore. I even start to cringe when I enter my key into the lock of the front door...."

Even though the actual topics of discussion will vary in every relationship, this is usually how the story goes. Two people meet. If the stars are aligned and the spark is present, they continue seeing each other. After a couple of dates, the butterflies in the stomach wake up from their dreadful winter sleep and our two love birds fall head-over-heels in love, get flooded with different hormones, neurotransmitters, and positive emotions. It's heaven on earth. Rainbow-tailed ponies and unicorns appear, and life is great. Their prayers have finally been answered, and Cupid has delivered a perfect match: a person without flaws. It may *really* seem that way.

Needless to say, when two people have just met they are both on their best behavior. Date night? Let's agonize over what to wear, clean the entire house, select great background music, light some candles, and make everything romantic. One lover cooked dinner? The other lover will, most probably, not spend the rest of the evening swiping on a phone or playing dead in front of the TV. Of course not! That lover will help clean up and will assist with loading the dishwasher (the right way). When we are trying to win the love of another person, no effort seems too big. The end justifies the means.

But then, when the two love birds happily move in together to start their ever-after, they enter uncharted territory in a strange new world where their many habits start to surface and *will* clash here and there. Where love is blind, moving in together turns out to be a very effective eye-opener. For some strange reason, *both* parties believed the other person would fully conform to *their* set of specific behaviors, habits, and wants. When that proves not to be the case, little irritations and points of friction unravel and the first arguments arise.

To some, this comes as a total shock. Understandable, given that it seemed like the other lover was totally devoted to them and would fully adapt without resistance. But now, out of nowhere, big challenges arise. Think of staring at an empty roll where the toilet paper used to live. Or wanting to watch the next episode of a favorite TV show together, only to hear: "I watched it when you were out last week." Dishwashers are loaded the wrong way; bathroom mirrors and sinks are in disarray. Snoring and sudden movements interrupt perfect dreams, and "how do I look?" no longer produces the desired answer. Clearly, none of these happened in the early stages of the relationship. In this strange new reality, frustrations may start to rise rapidly.

The Pivotal Shift

When you fall in love with someone, you'll feel like you've known them your entire life... even though you may have just met and only had a couple of dates together. Heck, some of us have had that feeling even though we didn't even know their last name. We're convinced that we've finally found someone who understands us and who loves us *unconditionally*.

However, once the pivotal shift occurs, the fog of love lifts and real life comes knocking at the door again. That's when some of us, especially those who forgot to do everything I'm covering in this book, come to a startling conclusion: "I don't know you at all!"

Both parties want to change one another, but they are often using the wrong strategies. As the annoyances progressively rise and continue over the long term, some couples start to feel unloved. That's an alarming moment because if this lasts, their gaze, for the first time, is turned outward—away from the relationship. They no longer enjoy the company of their lover and feel empty instead. Rather than work on the relationship, one or both parties start to look for what else is out there. Consequently, they may develop feelings for someone else. When these feelings prove to be reciprocal, the original relationship is abandoned, and everything starts over with a new person. According to the French philosopher Voltaire, divorce was invented around the same time as marriage. About six weeks later to be precise.

Now, of course, the very same problems will arise with the new partner because no attention was paid to what went wrong in the first place. Only this time, the shelf life of the new relationship may even be shorter. Marriages are the only form of relationships where we can statistically measure the duration, and according to the National Center for Family and Marriage Research from Bowling Green State University, 50 percent of all marriages end in divorce. That's a lot. However, 60 percent of second marriages and 65 percent of third and fourth marriages also end in divorce. These are all examples of people who should have learned from their mistakes. They probably didn't even become aware of the root cause of their relationship's demise. They presumably believed, "My current partner is no longer giving me what I need, so let me exchange them for a new one." But our partners are not an empty bottle of hand sanitizer we can simply replace.

Consequently, these people just keep repeating the same mistakes in each of their relationships.

The hormones and neurotransmitters we feel when we fall for someone give us a head start. It's nature's way of telling us we could very well match with that attractive person. Yet we shouldn't be fooled. That type of love is blind and portrays a very unrealistic perspective. The rainbow-tailed ponies and unicorns we see on that love cloud should give us a clue, but love actually *is* blind. Scientists have proven that love partially shuts down the critical and analytical part of our brain.[1] Furthermore, neurotransmitters and hormones like oxytocin cause us to label the other person as "the perfect partner" *and* evaluate them more positively than they may actually be, as proven by a multitude of studies.[2] Our image of our love interest doesn't mesh with reality. It's then up to us to make sure we are *really* dealing with a compatible partner and if so, turn hormonal love into mature, lasting love—not exactly an easy task.

Just as a power plant doesn't come with electricity and needs to make it, a good long-term relationship doesn't come with love and needs to generate it. Feeling loved and meeting needs are often effortless in the first few weeks of falling in love thanks to the chemical cocktail our bodies prepare for us. However, it requires effort from both parties to avoid failing in love.

---

[1] Neuroimage. 2004 Mar;21(3):1155-66. The neural correlates of maternal and romantic love. Bartels A[1], Zeki S.

[2] Front. Behav. Neurosci., 11 March 2014 | https://doi.org/10.3389/fnbeh.2014.00068, Catherine Crockford, Tobias Deschner, Toni E. Ziegler, Roman M. Wittig

Empty Love Ponds

Don't worry. There is light at the end of the tunnel, and it isn't from an oncoming train. Rachel and Brad, the couple that I started this chapter off with, have their happy ending for now. They're still together and have considerably increased their happiness in the relationship. The safety has been restored, and Brad is now a proud member of the Eye-Rolling Anonymous group; he hasn't done it for ages. He changed his ways just as much as Rachel has. They are a team, after all. I won't go into the details yet, but this was a classic case of filling up the wrong love ponds. Brad was a nest-builder (one of the love ponds), meaning that bringing home money to build a great nest for his girl and eventually the kids were his primary motivator. He lived for it. It was his way of showing how much he loved his girlfriend. He truly *was* working hard for her every single day.

However, this was not an important love pond to Rachel, so he was filling up the wrong pool. She didn't care that much about the nest yet. That's why she felt unloved. Rachel, on the other hand, was making some major mistakes as well. Given that nest-building was Brad's most important pond, she was doing a pretty dismal job at showing her love for him. She wasn't really helping out in that area, and furthermore, she was *hindering* him from taking care of what was essential to his love pond. What's the solution in a case like this? Figuring out the empty love ponds of each other, bringing out the love hose, and putting an end to the negativity. That's exactly what they did.

In my experience, all of the seven love ponds matter. We shouldn't just focus on one of them, not even two! They all eventually dry out—some just a lot faster than others, and these require a lot more attention. Yet we need to be mindful of *all of them*. None of them should ever be empty because an empty love pond creates disrespectful and unloving behavior in return!

Another great analogy for this love pond concept is looking at houseplants. They also need some of your love and attention in order to survive and thrive. If you don't water them or give them fertilizer, they won't make it. However, not all plants need the same amount of water and nourishment. In my house, I have plants that I need to water twice a week, others just once a week, and some even only once every couple of months. All of your lover's ponds will need attention (so do yours), just not at the same frequency and intensity.

When relationships start to fail, it's always because of a lack of love and an increase in hostility and negativity. The safety will have vanished. The love climate must be restored via the love ponds as soon as possible. This is challenging because if a certain pond is not important to you personally, you're instinctively not going to give it a great deal of attention, even though that may very well be exactly your partner's pond that is desperately crying for your attention.

Feeling Safe in Your Relationship

Great relationships are all about safety. If there is no safety, there is no relationship.

Trust comes when you are allowed to be yourself without judgment, attack, criticism, misunderstanding, or being ignored. When there is a never-ending flow of love coming your way, you'll know you are safe. When you know that the relationship matters as much to your lover as it does to you, a fundamental need is met. And even though you may not yet have thought of it that way, this is a safety we've all been looking for from the moment we were born. We want to be loved deeply for who we are, not who we pretend to be.

"I'm not really looking forward to it," Brenda said as she was applying some final makeup in front of the passenger side mirror in her boyfriend Mike's car.

She was very nervous and uncomfortable, that much was obvious.

"Why? What's going on?" Mike asked.

"I don't know anybody in your company. And I'm honored that you've invited me to your office party, but I'm afraid I won't have anyone to talk to. And if you run away to talk to colleagues, I'll be standing there on my own, all alone. And I'm not good at that," Brenda clarified as she nervously fidgeted with her dress. She felt ridiculous and didn't like the fact that she was so open about her insecurities so soon in their relationship, but she couldn't help it. She had to think of previous traumas where other boyfriends had disappeared for more than an hour, leaving her all alone while she had to fend off drunk colleagues that tried to hit on her and had to

27

talk to people she didn't have anything in common with. She was never a social star, and social events like these made her nervous.

"Baby, I won't leave your side," Mike assured her. "You can take my arm or hand and not let go for the entire night. I won't mind. Cling on to me. I'll make sure I introduce you to everyone we meet and if you feel like you're not having fun, let me know and we'll get out of there right away. Does that sound like a good plan?"

It did to Brenda, who felt relieved; and Mike kept his word. He looked out for her the entire evening. Brenda felt safe and protected, and she had fun.

Now if Mike doesn't suffer from any form of social anxiety, he may not have understood Brenda's concerns. He could have thought: "When you stand somewhere alone, you just find someone to talk to. Piece of cake! Other people don't bite! What's the big deal?" He could have reacted badly and told Brenda she was overreacting. But he didn't. Mike wanted Brenda to feel safe. Even though he didn't share her fear, he understood it and was there for her the entire night. When Brenda feels fearful, he drops everything and comes over to help. She would do the same for him. That's what safety in a relationship is all about.

This is only one of the many examples of how a relationship can bring us safety, a "you and me against the world" feeling. "We're in this together" is what people in successful relationships always apply.

Over the years, I've consulted over a thousand people to figure out what made their relationships work. I once took interviews in a retirement home and asked couples, widows, and widowers who had been *happily* married for over forty years for their secrets. Even though they all used different words, safety and their bond were the common threads in their examples. One of their tricks I discovered was that they knew very well how to communicate and act in a loving way that always protected that feeling of safety between them.

In their book *Crucial Conversations*, researchers and experts Kerry Patterson and Joseph Grenny stress that when we have a crucial conversation with someone, be that in or outside of our romantic relationship, safety is the most important pillar. As soon as a conversation feels unsafe, meaning we sense that the other party doesn't seem to care about our wellbeing, we will probably raise our voice or withdraw. That's why many people don't get what they want when they request something from their lover. They do so in such a way that feels unsafe and unloving to their partner. When, however, we create safety within our conversations and prove we care about the other person's feelings and needs, it's possible to talk about anything and get our message across fully.

It's our job to know what matters to our loved ones, to provide it for them, and to make them feel safe within the relationship. They, of course, need to do the same for us. If this, as silly and basic as it may sound, is not present, then the relationship will generate more worries and arguments than it can handle, and the exit sign will start to flash.

The seven love ponds you're about to discover in a couple of chapters will help bring that safety to the relationship. The good news is that it's easier than you may think. But before I can explain the different love ponds, we'll need to lay the groundwork first.

The Promised Land and the Holy Grail

You've spent months, possibly years, going on dates with strangers. Your finger may have needed bed rest from all that swiping through hundreds of profiles on a dating app, trying to find a match. Or you did it the old-fashioned way and approached attractive strangers with a pounding heart as if you were about to hand-feed a juicy hot dog to an alligator. You've spent money trying to look nice for that person. You possibly worked out extra hard to look your best. You've ditched friends and dialed down on time spent on your favorite hobbies. You've done *a lot,* and you've given up even more just to be in a loving relationship with that person.

And you finally arrived in the Promised Land! All went well in the beginning. But for some reason, you started to feel a hunger. Something was missing. Thoughts like "if he could just be a little bit more..." and "I would love it if she would just..." started to pop up. The first unmet needs. And don't worry, you were *both* thinking those first little thoughts of friction.

We all have needs, and deep down, our subconscious brain is indeed looking for the Holy Grail: unconditional love and the unconditional fulfillment of *all* of our needs and dreams. It's our birthright, so it believes. In order to get it, we may follow some less than ideal strategies. Think of the man who behaves distantly and even withdraws whenever his girlfriend tries to come close. He clearly doesn't want to hold hands and most definitely doesn't want to cuddle. He's apparently very cold and seemingly has fewer emotions than your average psychopath. Yet all he wants *is* to be loved and to be close to someone (including the hand-holding and the cuddling). In a very childish move nevertheless, our man here has pushed that more sensitive part of him very far away because of bad experiences with past girlfriends where he *had* opened up, where he became "soft," only to get burned after. He is still licking his sore wounds. This guy will definitely not get the love he wants because of his aloofness, and he *will* make the woman he's with utterly miserable.

Indeed, the woman who is in a relationship with such a man wonders what's going on. She tries to unlock the vault; she attempts to change him. She believes that deep down he must be a good man. She says things like, "Why don't you ever hug me?" and "You used to be more affectionate. Don't you love me anymore?" in an effort to open him up. And even though these are very valid needs to have, she now comes across as needy (according to him) and thus pushes him away even further. She won't get what she wants either.

Nobody wins in this game. When needs are not getting met in a relationship, the frustrations rise on both sides because both parties have invested so much of their time and efforts in each other. Was it all for nothing? Our woman here may think, "How could he not give me what I need? I do *everything* for him! And all I ask in return is for him to be more affectionate, but he withholds that from me. I can't believe it! I would *never* do that to him!" We can't blame her.

And thus, the infamous power struggle starts.
The relationship starts to look like a battlefield *or* becomes so quiet and passionless that it now has tumbleweeds blowing through it.

But here's the kicker. These two would be perfect for each other! They have the same needs (being cozy, loving, cuddly, affectionate). They just don't seem to realize it because for some reason they both fail to openly share what they *really* need to feel loved and when they do try to communicate about it, they do so in such a way that makes the other person feel unsafe. The messages they want to send to one another are deflected, blocked, and otherwise not received. They are trying to get their needs met in the wrong way, often because of past wounds that are still acting out.

Some seemingly harmless behaviors can have a ripple effect within relationships. "Coming on too strong" is another great example. It usually scares the other party away, man or woman. We all know that. Yet it's a mistake that's easy to be made because of the infatuation we feel when we've just fallen for someone. Love and infatuation can indeed make us lose control. But at the same time, there's an interesting concept at play here. Most women, for instance, understand that it's generally a bad idea to bring up the topic of marriage and baby names over a piña colada during the first date. But some women believe they have to continuously keep what they want to themselves, even though they are in a long-term relationship. They *still* keep quiet, scared of pushing the one they love away. And in doing so, they lower their value within that relationship, some even to doormat level. We are entitled to have our own unique preferences and needs. It's OK that they are and probably *will* be different than those of our partner.

We have a fundamental right to feel fulfilled. If we're in a real relationship and we don't get our needs met, then we have indeed been communicating our needs in the wrong way. We may have been pushing too hard; we may have shown needy behavior all along, making our lover hesitant. In this case, the problem is not *that* we communicate about our needs; it's *how* we do it. You'll get plenty of examples of what to and not to do in the next chapters. Or we've picked the wrong lover, and they have no intention of ever putting in the effort to make us happy. They'd rather arm-wrestle a hungry lion than to ever fulfill our needs. It happens... both sexes tend to date and relate to people they have no future with. And because people who are bad for us are usually not followed around by a swarm of flies, we tend to miss it at first. It's only natural.

That's not what this book is about though. If we're with the wrong person, we have no reason for being with them. In what follows, I'm going to presuppose that you've picked the right partner, but that for some reason, your needs remain unmet. And whatever it is you try, it seems to only widen the distance between the both of you.

There is a solution to this predicament. But for that solution to work, we first need to understand love. It's a word that's handed out like candy, but there's a lot more to it than sweetness.

Love, the Most Ambiguous Word in the Dictionary

After getting air, water, food, and maybe a high-speed Internet connection, feeling loved is the most important need most people are trying to meet. There's no better feeling on earth than knowing someone we have feelings for chooses to love us.

That last sentence reveals an important formula in which every element is important.

1. Knowing
2. Someone we have feelings for
3. Chooses to love us

They are all indispensable. First, we have to know that the other person loves us. It has to *feel* like love and be sincere. As we'll see over and over again, someone who expresses their love by pouring water into the wrong love pond will not make us feel loved however hard they are trying. Someone who's not sufficiently interested or doesn't mean well won't make us feel loved either. We'll feel in our gut that something is off, given that it won't feel like genuine love.

Second, we need to have feelings for that person. I'm sure you have known people who were "in love" with you, but you couldn't care less. You may have taken it as a compliment, you may have found it awkward, but you didn't feel that tingly fulfilling sensation that real love brings us.

Third, one that is often overlooked, it has to be a *choice*.

The best kind of love is the one where we know, deep down, that the other person is putting in an effort to make us feel loved. It's their deliberate choice; our lover is investing in us and in our relationship, and we don't have to nag, manipulate, play games, threaten to leave, or hold their favorite pet for ransom. Our lover does it by choice. That's genuine, mature love—the best kind. We'll go over plenty of examples in the rest of this book, but think back to the guy who promised he wouldn't leave his girlfriend's side the entire evening at his office party. It doesn't come naturally to him to stay by her side; he chooses to do that for her *and* she chooses to face her fears for him. She isn't great at being extroverted and meeting new people, yet there she was by his side. These are acts of love, and that's why they feel so good.

Imagine a woman who dearly loves her husband. They have been married for eleven years, and she knows he's having a tough time at work with the occurrence of layoffs. His pink slip may come anytime now. As her husband arrives home one night, she asks him to sit down next to her on the couch. She places one hand on his knee and lays his hand on hers. She says, "John, I know you're having a hard time at work. But I want to tell you I'm proud of you. The past fourteen years that we've known each other, I've always been so proud to be your lady. Every day of the week, you go out and work hard for us. I try to do the same, but knowing I have you and you're taking this job uncertainty so well gives me the strength to keep going. I'm proud to be your wife, and I'm glad I've married such a strong man, regardless of what happens with your job."

Have you pictured it? How is John feeling now? Do you think this helps? It probably will. If, and that's an important if, his wife knows his love ponds well enough, this will help out significantly. He will feel loved and supported and even if only for a moment, he'll forget his job worries. When John hugs and kisses his wife following this talk, how will she feel? She will feel loved in return if John doesn't forget to look after her most important love ponds either. Why wouldn't he? She just made him feel like the king of the world. All great kings love to take care of their queen. They are a perfect team.

This conversation was not an accidental one. It didn't happen by chance or because of hormones. The wife in this example knows very well what John needs to feel loved, to feel nurtured. She could have made him a five-course dinner and surprised him with tickets for next week's football game while wearing her revealing white lace nightgown... she could have done a lot of things that would have made absolutely no difference to John. But she *knows* him, and he knows her.

They both understand that fulfilling our deep emotional needs for love is what we all strive for. When the need is not fulfilled, we feel unstable. John felt unstable at work; she made sure he could feel stable at home. It was a choice, her loving choice—one that John makes every day as well.

Having our needs taken care of is not only what brings the romance to the relationship, it's the glue that makes it last. Knowing that someone wants us and genuinely loves us so much that they are willing to put in the effort of giving us what we *specifically* need *is* feeling loved.

And there's no better way to feel loved than to make sure the love ponds are nicely filled. Here they are.

The First Love Pond

"It's not going so well," Marissa told me a couple of years ago. "Bryce is getting more and more distant. I'm not even sure he still loves me. He did, but something has changed. We haven't been intimate in over four months, and it was only because *I* initiated it. He always used to take the lead, but he no longer does. He also stopped helping out at home, he's away from home more often, he doesn't have time for me, so it seems. Do you think he's seeing someone else, Brian? Does he still love me? What can I do to make him love me the way I love him?"

I could feel the fear in her voice.

"Are *you* different now?" I asked.

"Yes," Marissa admitted. "I complain more, and I'm starting to get fed up with his inaction and withdrawal. It just hurts so much that he's not willing to put in the effort to take care of my needs."

Situations like these are always interesting. In general, there are two possibilities. Either her boyfriend Bryce is a total jerk who couldn't care less about what Marissa wants. If she were chased by a herd of angry buffalos, he would grab a beer and enjoy the show. Or Marissa is, at least in part, making Bryce act out this way. Let's find out.

"So what have you tried to do about it?" I wondered, trying to figure out Bryce's empty love pond.

"I tell it to him. I'm trying to change him. I've already told him that the husbands and boyfriends of all my friends *do* spend more time with their girlfriends and wives. I'm not that demanding, he's just lazy. He even stopped helping out in and around the house, and when he did help out before, it was never up to standard. The other day friends invited us over, and as we were given a tour of their beautifully remodeled house, I complimented Marc, my friend, for everything he has done there. I even jokingly said Bryce no longer does anything at home and that he should get a raise so we can pay someone else instead to upgrade our house. You know, just to give a hint."

"So how did he respond?" I asked.

"He became even more distant. He didn't say a word on the drive home."

"And do you try to change other things about him as well?" I wondered.

"Yes, I'm not very fond of things like his clothing style either."

"How do you make that clear to him?" I asked.

"I bought him what I would like him to wear as a gift for Christmas. And I have to say, his family agreed that he should make some changes."

The conversation continued down that path with more examples of how Marissa tried to "encourage" Bryce, until I concluded: "So, Marissa, am I correct in understanding that you would love to change Bryce and that you tell him often? That you try to get others to help you in convincing him he should change? That, *even* when he helps out and does something for you, it's never really good enough? That you claim he doesn't work hard enough or doesn't earn enough, *even publicly?* In other words, are you regularly making it clear you don't really *value* Bryce for who he is now? Could he be getting the feeling that you're trying to *fix* him because he's broken?"

"Umm yes... I guess so," Marissa acknowledged, slowly starting to realize that she was not on the right track here. I could almost see the light bulbs going off in her head. So many of them in fact that she started to look like a Christmas tree. Her approach, used by many people nonetheless, is as successful as trying to convince an Amish farmer to trade his horse in for a Lamborghini.

Even though it will be obvious to you, Marissa was unaware that she had been *attacking* Bryce all along; she even did it publicly with the help of her friends and family. Everyone against Bryce. When Bryce did help out, it was never good enough. Bryce's opinion was often not considered. He was also apparently not earning enough, and she made it clear (publicly) he didn't take care of her. Bryce clearly needed to be fixed and fast.

Why wouldn't he withdraw then? How could Bryce possibly feel valuable, important, and safe in their relationship when he was regularly put down or ignored? Marissa made him feel insignificant. Mind you, Bryce was not a drunk-before-noon slacker or a slough. He was a hard-working and kind guy who was doing the best he could. While trying to make a "better" man out of him, Marissa had turned her prince into a frog. Even though he really was a good guy, that buffalo chase probably started to sound like less of a bad idea the more these put-downs continued.

When we are compared to others, criticized, ignored, made to feel inadequate; when our needs, wants, wishes, opinions, and personal values are frowned upon or blatantly dismissed; when our lover doesn't prioritize us or makes us feel insignificant in any way; when our boundaries are ignored or when our partner's behavior toward us is inconsiderate; when praise and admiration are mostly absent, alarm bells go off. They should! When these behaviors are egregious or when many of them are combined, anyone would feel unloved. Yet for some, even a *subtle hint* of any of these is all it takes to empty our first love pond.

You may already have guessed it, but the first love pond I want to discuss is called **respect**. I understand I sound like Captain Obvious right now. Obviously, *everyone* wants to be respected in a relationship. The late Aretha Franklin has been singing it since 1967. R.E.S.P.E.C.T is vital, and it is indeed a cornerstone of every loving relationship. As I said, all of the love ponds matter greatly, but the layout, the importance, and *especially* the sensitivity of the love ponds make all the difference. Some people don't need much to feel respected; others need you to tediously care for this particular love pond. They will not only need loads of respect, *tiny subtle hints* of disrespect hurt them greatly.

In Bryce's case, small remarks or "jokes" made the water evaporate in no time, *especially* when they are made in public. The lack of praise, approval, and positive feedback weren't helping either. What really did it, however, was that Bryce didn't seem to have any value to Marissa. He *mistakenly* believed he was totally insignificant to her and found plenty of proof in her actions. Bryce was convinced Marissa didn't like who he was because she kept stacking little signs of disrespect upon one another. Even though Marissa's remarks were meant as well-meaning and friendly hints because she loved him and wanted to bring out the best in him, they hit Bryce's fragile ego like a nuclear torpedo. Marissa was a loving girlfriend in many forms and did a lot for Bryce, she just happened to ignore the *one* love pond that mattered most.

When we feel insignificant, taken for granted or disrespected, it will be very difficult to show love to our partner. People like Bryce, however, need very little to feel disrespected. This was a powerfully vicious cycle for Bryce and Marissa. Even though Marissa's mistake will seem very obvious when you read her story, it started out very innocently. What we saw here was just the end game. Her early, very subtle signs of disrespect already made Bryce withdraw and crawl into his shell. She, consequently sensing even *less* love coming from him, upped the ante. That's when the train derailed.

Nevertheless, Bryce is not the only victim here. As we'll discover later, he's doing a fine job at blatantly ignoring one of Marissa's more important love ponds and is just as guilty. That's why he pushed Marissa toward disrespectful behavior. He was totally unaware of the fact that *he* brought on her disrespectful behavior at least partially. The more unloved she felt, the more she lost respect for him and started acting out. They were both starting to bring out the worst in each other, instead of the best. When problems arise in relationships, the love ponds are very often at play. Instead of focusing on attacking or ignoring each other, Bryce and Marissa needed to focus on the love ponds.

People with a sensitive respect love pond need to feel significant to their lover and will be *very* sensitive to inconsiderate behavior. They need to rest assured that they are important and their partner supports them and is proud to be with them. They will be very sensitive to signs that prove otherwise. They need to know, without a shadow of a doubt, they are loved for who they are.

And I repeat, all of this will be important to *everyone*, yet for some people this particular love pond is really fragile. Whereas someone with a not so sensitive respect pond can, for example, handle you poking fun (even in public), to someone sensitive like Bryce it feels like public emasculation. No kidding.

Some people don't mind when you make plans that involve them without asking for their consent. Others, those with a sensitive respect pond, will believe it's indispensable you consult with them first. Some people can do just fine without regular support and praise of their lover; others need it as a vital lifeline. Some don't care when they are judged by their lover and appreciate the feedback; others feel their self-confidence shrink dramatically. Some people don't mind when plans are cancelled; others will see it as a major sign of disrespect. Some people won't care when they are not a significant priority of their lover; others will feel unloved quickly. All of these are directly linked to the sensitivity of the respect pond.

Marissa's ignorance of Bryce's very sensitive love pond had consequences. When someone feels hurt or doesn't feel loved because of an empty love pond, they will either become angry and retaliate (while often becoming disrespectful themselves), or they withdraw. That's exactly what happened to Bryce; he withdrew. The more Marissa tried to "encourage" Bryce by telling him how all of the other husbands were better than him, the more she was in fact pushing him away into a gridlock. It just emptied his batteries and sucked the life out of him, so he withdrew and became complacent. That response made it look like he just didn't care, yet he cared *a lot,* much more than Marissa ever imagined.

Interestingly, previous boyfriends of Marissa had responded favorably to that treatment. Because they didn't have such a sensitive respect pond, they saw those comparisons with others as a challenge. It motivated them into action. That's what makes the concept of this book so interesting. What worked well on previous partners you've had may no longer work on the current one. We all come with different wiring and a very personal user manual.

A Pretty Interesting Experiment

I told Marissa about a remarkable experiment a scientist called Dr. Goldstein had performed. In short, he looked for angry and neglected wives whose husbands cheated and actually left the household to move in with the new flame. Could Dr. Goldstein, for the sake of science, get those husbands to come back with their tails between their legs? Given that these angry women were getting nowhere with their current approach, they were more than happy to give this a chance. We'll leave whether or not these women *should* have taken their husbands back out of the equation; getting them back is what they wanted.

One wife in particular, let's call her Sabrina, presented an interesting case. After years of being in an unhappy marriage, Sabrina's husband finally left her... to move in with his new girlfriend. Interestingly enough, he kept calling Sabrina every now and then to see how she was. So he clearly still had somewhat of an interest in her. This is obviously crucial.

Now the question was, could Sabrina, for the sake of this experiment, influence the behavior of her ex-husband after he had already left her? The strategy was to behave differently than she had during the marriage. This time, she would reward good behavior by giving compliments and stay indifferent to bad behavior. She was going to "respect" him lavishly. I'm sure you can sense how counterintuitive this approach is. "A traitor's feelings shouldn't be spared," Sabrina believed. But for this experiment, she was prepared to forgo her belief.

The first goal was to see if she could increase the frequency of his calls to her. Sabrina never reached out to him; she was always on the receiving end. When he did call, she was very affectionate and positive. She praised the things she *did* like about him and neglected what she didn't like (e.g., the fact that he left her after many years of marriage to move in with a new girlfriend). Sabrina meticulously recorded everything that happened—when he called, for how long, what they talked about, and more.

She was never critical, hostile, or negative, and she always made sure that *she* was the one ending the calls. It didn't take long before the frequency of the phone calls increased significantly.

One day, he arrived at her house. Following the plan of the experiment, Sabrina said, "I'm so glad you're here. I have a fresh, imported Cuban cigar for you in the freezer, just the kind you like."

Sabrina continued to reinforce his good behavior (everything she liked) and paid no attention to the negative behavior. That very negative behavior, like his indifference, melted away *automatically*, and it didn't take long before he left his new girlfriend and asked if he could move back in.

This is a very interesting experiment, isn't it? At first glance, it may seem that Sabrina kneeled for her cheating husband, started to treat him like a king even though he deserved the moldy dungeon, and that this is just silly. Why would you treat anyone who is not treating you well or not fulfilling your needs like a king? As it happens, this was the very key to rekindling his love for her and happily making him treat her like the queen she was. After all, we love being around someone who makes us feel good; it's really that simple.

As we saw a few chapters back, when a relationship becomes drenched in negativity, criticism, and complaints, at least one of the parties will start to look for greener grass elsewhere. When the positive atmosphere is restored, the relationship often heals. Sabrina had played a role in what had gone wrong before, just as she played a role now while restoring it. The cold hard truth is that if we have picked the right partner and the relationship still goes south, we sometimes had a hand in the change of direction. And that's the good news, given that we may be able to undo it and restore the relationship.

To fix certain relationships *that are worth fixing*, we will often have to give first. I've seen this play out repeatedly, and Bryce and Marissa, the couple I started this chapter with, were no different.

As soon as Marissa started to pay attention to what was important to Bryce (allowing him to be Bryce, mostly, and thus respecting him for who he was while giving him some additional praise here and there), he felt loved again. He started to heal and began to feel like a real man once more. His very sensitive ego mended. Consequently, the giving back started. He took care of her needs now, without Marissa asking for it. Surprisingly, he even started to wear some of the clothes Marissa liked more than his current style. Not because she nagged about it, this time *he* wanted to as a token of his love for her. It truly was as if Marissa had given him a superhero pill. Now, feeling respected, it was much easier for Bryce to care for Marissa's needs in return. *And* he started to come on to her in the bedroom like he did in the past. This too had just been a consequence of what had happened. Bryce no longer felt like a man, given that Marissa had continuously been putting him down during her efforts of changing him. Some will say Bryce is too sensitive, but his sensitivity doesn't matter. Bryce is who he is. He didn't get to choose the sensitivity of his own love ponds. That's the result of his upbringing, the way his parents treated him, his personality and genes, and so on. Think back to the safety we discussed. We can only blossom when we are allowed to be who we are in our relationship and when our partner loves us for everything we are *and* everything we are not. Great relationships are a secure refuge where we can be ourselves. We don't judge shortcomings or differences, we can only choose whether we accept them or not. And if we don't, then there is no relationship.

Luckily, situations like these are easy to fix once you understand what's going on. Even if Marissa had been cooking him dinner in a sexy blouse, taking him on vacations the jet set doesn't even get to experience, giving him the reins of the TV remote at all times... none of that would have mattered. As long as the leak in the respect pond wasn't plugged, Bryce's behavior wouldn't have changed much. That's why Marissa was so frustrated when she sought me out. She was trying to be a good girlfriend, just not in the way that mattered most to Bryce. All Marissa had to do was demonstrate that she respected and appreciated Bryce, that she cared for his feelings, and that she loved him for who he was, flaws included. He, obviously, gave her the very same treatment in return.

In general, all types of behaviors that prove that a lover is important to the other person will fill the respect pond. All types of behaviors that seem to prove the lover is insignificant, empty it by the boatload.

Respect and Love

Respect and love are intricately connected in an interesting way. Let's say a woman feels disrespected by her boyfriend or husband. She, in turn, will find it really hard to love *him* and give him what he needs. The man, on the other hand, now also feeling unloved, will find it even harder to respect his woman. A negative vicious cycle gets started. Love and disrespect do not match, but the absence of one generates the other. The absence of love generates disrespect. The absence of disrespect creates room for love to grow.

When a man feels disrespected, he will stop giving signs of love and will increase signs of hostility. In other words, he now becomes unloving. He may turn silent and withdraw, snap, become cynical, or attack in any other hurtful way. Interestingly, *he now becomes disrespectful himself.* His lady promptly feels even more unloved, thus making her *more* disrespectful... and the vicious cycle keeps going round and round.

So if disrespect exists, we need to wonder why! The respect might never have been there from the get-go. In that case, we've chosen the wrong partner. But chances are it *was* abundant in the beginning and then slowly started to erode. When that takes place, we have to look for unmet needs or other love ponds in trouble. When our partner acts disrespectfully, it may indeed be because they feel unloved themselves.

Even good people become disrespectful when they are hurting and losing their all-important connection. This is an important mind shift. When we receive a disrespectful reaction from our lover, we feel hurt and will automatically focus on how *bad* the other person is. That's a gut-level response because our feelings were hurt. However, we need to step back and look for what WE might have done wrong to deserve it.

Respect is a given in every relationship with fully filled love ponds, a good bond, and lots of safety. If we were receiving respect and it suddenly stops, we need to find out what happened. Focus on the love ponds and the level of negativity present, and use what follows to make things right again. The respect should then return. If you're the one who needs this pond filled, then remember that being unloving breeds disrespectful behavior. Also understand that in many relationships, disrespectful behavior was *not* intended as such; it's merely perceived that way. As I've said, this book presupposes that you've selected a great person to be in a relationship with.

If you sense that your lover's respect pond needs a refill, then prove your lover is important to you and do so without conditions. Don't think: "I'll be respectful as soon as my lover makes me feel loved or as soon as my companion appreciates how much I love him or her." Remember the vicious cycle. We have to be respectful without conditions or there is no relationship in the first place. Here are a few practices you can implement:

- Even if you disagree or disapprove, respect your lover's wishes, opinions, and boundaries.
- Be proud of your lover's achievements and tell him or her often.

- Make your partner one of your priorities. (e.g. If you make decisions that have an impact on your partner, ask for your partner's opinion. When your partner wants to talk about something, but you feel you have more important things to do, make time. If you have to choose between disappointing a friend or a family member *or* your partner, don't disappoint your partner.)
- Tell your partner why you respect him or her, and be specific.
- Give praise. Focus on what your lover does well, what you like about your lover, and try to be specific.
- Demonstrate your confidence in their decisions.
- Prove that you value their efforts, and *tell* your lover.

In general: make your lover feel important.

I'll dive into the details later on, but needless to say, we do all of this as a strong person—never as a needy doormat craving approval. Even if we have to give first, we do so as a mature and empowered person, and we don't keep on giving endlessly if we're not valued for who we are in return. Respect is a two-way street.

The Second Love Pond

Let's now look at Jess and Sam. They have been together for twelve years but if you'd sit at the table next to them in a restaurant, you'd speculate whether it was their second date. They're so playful you'd wonder what their secret is.

Sam has just spilled his drink, and it's all over the table. Jess helps clean it up, and as they both sit back down she looks at him with a hard-to-hide grin on her face.

"What?" Sam says.

"You're so adorable and goofy," Jess replies, trying not to laugh. "I think I'm going to have to subtract points from the 'knows how to take me to a classy dinner' scorecard. But don't worry, I'm sure you'll figure out a way to make it up to me later tonight."

As Jess winks, Sam takes her hand and tries to maintain his serious face as long as possible. "I knew you were trouble the moment I met you. I've given it a lot of thought, and... I think we should start seeing other people."

Now they both start to laugh out loud.

"You're absolutely right," Jess assures. "By the way, did I tell you I'm starting a writing class next week?" and now Jess starts to passionately talk about a new endeavor she's partaking in, as Sam listens and wonders how he got so lucky to have found such a great woman twelve years ago.

Sam and Jess are no different at home. If you were a fly on the wall, you'd be surprised at how playful they still are at times, especially when it matters most. Sam just came home from a hard day at work and decided to relax and plant himself on the couch to watch some TV, leaving an uninteresting mail trail from the front door to the kitchen table as well as a half-eaten apple on the countertop. Not to mention, he forgot to take off his dirty shoes, leaving a muddy path that made the living room look like a cow had just plowed through it.

Jess arrives home a bit later, and she's a tad surprised to see the mess. She has had a tough day as well and cleaning all of this up is the absolute last thing on her mind. Do you know what else is last on her mind? Complaining and nagging. So with a smile, she says, "Hey honey, did you forget to mention you took a home-study rodeo course? Are you secretly a cowboy? There's dirt all over the place. I always knew you were special, honey. Why don't you show me what kind of a superman you are by cleaning this mess up while I change into something more comfortable? Then we can prepare dinner in a clean house. You know how I love a clean house, right?" and off she goes to the bedroom.

As she comes back wearing just a sweater and some sweatpants, Sam is finalizing the big cleanup. Even though a clean house apparently isn't that important to him, Jess has already made it clear in the past that she won't tolerate a messy place. She never nagged about it; she just made it loud and clear with statements like: "I love you, and I know cleanliness isn't that important to you, but it is to me. And I want to be with a man who respects me enough to help me keep the house clean. I hope you can be that man for me, Sam. I would love for it to be you; otherwise, I have to go back to looking at all of those dating profiles of men who will talk about how much money they make. Men who will compliment my eyes while staring at my bosom. Is that really what you want to put me through, Sam? Is it really?" (All said with a smile, of course.)

Are you already on to what the second love pond is?

It isn't cleanliness. It's fun—actual, good old-fashioned playful fun. It's all about positive energy. In other words, it's the opposite of negativity. Negativity is toxic and ruins relationships. It's a true Trojan horse. Some people "welcome" negativity in while being oblivious to its long-term effects. As research has proven, it takes multiple positive events to cancel out one negative event.[3] Scientists even have a name for the underlying system: negativity bias. The more negativity there is, no matter what form, the more the foundation of the relationship (the bond) will erode. Flirting, unpredictability, teasing, and playfulness, on the other hand, are part of love's energy sources. It can generate and regenerate love for as long as you want. I've personally seen many couples restore their relationship by paying attention to just this love pond in particular.

What do a lot of people who've just met do? They flirt. They tease. They have loads of fun. Their conversations are often playful instead of serious. They bring out the best in each other instead of the worst.

People who have been together for ages, on the other hand, are sometimes stuck in a rut, possibly no longer enjoy passionate love or flirting and may only talk about the practical to-dos of the household. If that's the case, fun has retired a long time ago. Their activities will also have become

---

[3] Gwendolyn Seidman, associate professor of psychology at Albright College in Reading, Penn in the article: Stop Complaining, it's ruining your relationships - Chicago Tribune February the 6th, 2017. http://chicagotribune.com/lifestyles/sc-couples-complain-family-0207-20170206-story.html - Furthermore, researcher John Gottman came to the same conclusions.

very predictable. Their relationship is far from what it looked like in their first couple of months together.

Fun is an important love pond to most people, but for some, it will be absolutely vital. And I want to stress that I'm not necessarily talking about balloons and childish clown-like fun. It's mostly the absence of negativity that counts. Having fun and being playful with each other fills this love pond; negativity makes the water vanish in an instant. It's hard to love a person who's regularly negative about us or who makes us feel bad. And as obvious as this may sound, a lot of people seem to forget about this very straightforward concept once they are in a relationship. Think back to Marissa from the first love pond. She tried to use *negativity* to get her needs met, and we saw how effective that strategy was.

Jess and Sam are a great example of how fun can be incorporated into the most mundane events. In the restaurant, the flirting and playfulness brought the fun. At home when cowboy Sam got loose, Jess knew how to bring her disappointment with as little negativity as possible. Instead of attacking Sam for his sloppiness, she made it fun. In their case, fun (especially a lack of negativity) was a crucial love pond for Sam. While growing up, his parents had always been fighting, and as a result, he's very sensitive to negativity, raised voices, and fights in relationships—*even more so* than other people. They make him cringe and withdraw, just like he did when he was a kid.

If anything is wrong in a relationship, I always suggest looking for holes in the respect pond first and then come to this one. Relationships are supposed to be a voyage with unique and fun experiences that you can only have because of your relationship. It's true that the sun cannot shine every day and there will most definitely be storms to weather, but that makes it all the more important to deliberately care for this love pond. We are in control of what our relationship feels like. Always. We may not continually decide what happens, but we always choose how we respond to it. Even though the positive approach seems hard at first, it pays dividends and fast.

It's a pond, so fun doesn't have to be created *continuously*. Life is obviously serious too and the daily not-fun-at-all to-dos have to get done somehow. But fun and a lack of unnecessary negativity make us stronger and help us handle daily life much better. Look at it like an emotional bank account that shouldn't go into the red. You'll just need to make fun deposits every now and then and avoid negativity, which would make the balance plunge rapidly. Fun can both be added by activities *and* the way we choose to communicate. Both will matter greatly.

Fun activities and unique, unpredictable experiences can increase the attraction and love. In the beginning of the relationship, we go on terrifying adventures (also called first dates). We may feel so nervous we could lay an egg. These moments take us out of our comfort zone and give us feelings. At that phase, we take the time to surprise each other and to have positive and unpredictable experiences. Even flirting is about that unpredictability. It makes us feel alive, and that part doesn't need to end when you are in a long-term relationship. It's actually indispensable that it continues. Incorporating a monthly date night where you both dress up and go out is one example of the absolute minimum that will be required to look after this pond. But looking for other new experiences you could both share is another one.

I once coached two people well in their fifties who started to fill this love pond back up by going on one silly adventure every other weekend. That could be as simple as throwing a Frisbee in the park to visiting a museum even though the subject of the exposition was the last thing on their minds. These unpredictable experiences rekindled their bond between. Mini adventures where you both have fun *are* what created that bond in the first place. You may already have felt the difference between working with someone and then going on a trip with them. The combination of adventure and fun strengthen the bond in significantly different ways compared to working together in an office environment.

How we get those positive feelings and what fun looks like will be different for all of us. But the goal is to find something the both of you would enjoy and do more of that. This can go from playful banter or flirting to teasing messages to mini or even big adventures you both embark upon. It can be as silly as playing a fun board game instead of sitting in front of the TV all night. Try to add variety to your love life. Relationships are *not* meant to be a merry-go-round that keeps bringing us back to the same point over and over again. Life often takes over inconspicuously, and some of us forget all about this love pond, *especially* when there are kids running around. It's an easy love pond to fill up; the hard part is not forgetting about it.

Always make sure that the fun pond is sufficiently filled up by *avoiding negativity* directed toward each other as much as you can while *injecting* some moments of *playful fun* here and there, especially when you or your partner are highly sensitive to negativity and stress.

The Third Love Pond

"You're not there for me when I need it," a desperately frustrated Janice blamed Eric. They were both sitting in front of me. Eric had very reluctantly agreed to this conversation, given that, in his mind, he was not at all to blame, of course. At first sight, it indeed seemed like Eric was not doing anything wrong. The truth, however, would turn out to be quite the surprise for him.

Eric and Janice lived in a nice apartment, deliberately had no kids, and enjoyed vacations at least twice per year, often more. If you judged their relationship on their social media accounts featuring pictures of blissful love that would make the poster of your average romantic flick jealous, then everything was absolutely perfect between them. But under the hood, more than one part of the engine was misfiring, and dark smoke was starting to emerge from all sides. Their love engine was about to fall apart.

"Whenever I have a problem or just want to talk about my day, you don't seem to be listening. You just keep coming up with solutions, as if you want to sweep everything under the rug. You make me feel as if I'm exaggerating, as if I am making a big deal out of nothing. And whenever we have a discussion, it's always your way or the highway. You also think you're right, all the time, even when you're not. You can't seem to admit when you've got something wrong," Janice continued.

"No!" Eric interrupted firmly. "That is NOT true, *you* always..."

"Thank you for proving my point," Janice intervened while rolling her eyes.

"Do you have any goldfish?" I asked to break up their fight and cut short the destructive pattern they were in.

"Um yes… one. Why?" Janice replied with a surprised look on her face.

"Well, he must be getting quite the show when you perform this play at home. How many times per week is this show on?"

"We fight a lot lately indeed," Eric said with a defeated tone in his voice.

"And I understand why," I said. "This is a pattern, like a long-playing record that you just keep repeating. It has become your habit. It's a habit because you're *both* making the same mistake each and every time."

"What would that be then?" Janice wondered.

"You're directing your arrows at the wrong targets. You're attacking each other instead of the *real* cause, and you're both talking at a frequency that the other can't tune in to. Janice, do you still love Eric?"

"Of course, I do. That's why I'm so mad! I just don't understand why he can't seem to get that I just need him to be there for me."

"And you, Eric, do you still love Janice?"

"I sure do! I work hard every day, I often come home with flowers, I pay for those vacations we take, I compliment Janice's looks often, and I help out at home. I think, all things considered, I'm a pretty good boyfriend."

Eric honestly seemed to be a great guy indeed, yet the third love pond is starting to slowly emerge here. Can you see it?

It's the emotional empathy love pond. Even though Eric brings home flowers, compliments Janice, and pays for everything, he isn't emotionally present for Janice when she needs him the most. He's not connecting with her. This is a very important pond, given that it is so easy to get this one wrong.

The emotional empathy love pond stands for being the listening ear, for authentically connecting with our lover, for sharing the pain or the joy, for being in this together, for understanding (or at the very least trying to understand), for giving our partner the feeling that they are not alone to carry the weight of the emotional life that's put on either or both our shoulders. It's about the emotional burden indeed, not about helping out in the household for instance. (That would be a physical or practical aspect, and this pond is purely emotional.)

Eric was helping out in the household, paying for their vacations, trying to take care of his girlfriend as best as he could, but he was doing it in the wrong ways. Janice wanted a listening, understanding, and empathic ear *much more* than she needed those vacations. She wanted to connect with him and feel they were in this together, that he was there for her. And he wasn't, at least not in the way she needed him the most. There was nothing wrong with several other ponds, but there was anything but love in her emotional empathy pond.

Empathy

Empathy is a word and a concept that's misunderstood by a lot of people. I made a lot of empathy mistakes in my first relationships and even in the first years with my long-term girlfriend, and this particular pond happens to be her most important one, as it is for many women. You can imagine how much fun that was....

Theresa Wiseman Ph.D., a nursing scholar, did research on the four attributes of empathy and wrote a beautiful paper on the subject.[4] The four attributes are:

- The ability to see the world from the eyes of the other person, recognizing their perspective
- *To not judge that perspective*
- To recognize and understand the feelings of the other person
- To communicate that understanding to the other person

Empathy is about entering the circle the other person is standing in. It can be a circle of pain, of hurt, of sadness, of joy, of ecstasy. It's not about standing at the edge of the circle and just looking in. You'll need to join the other person *in* their circle if you want to make the connection.

It seems simple at first, but true empathy is hard in reality. Imagine a woman coming home with bad news. She just lost an important client at work, and it was her fault. The husband,

---

[4]https://www.researchgate.net/profile/Theresa_Wiseman/publication/ 234127308_Toward_a_holistic_conceptualisation_of_empathy_in_clinical _practice/links/0fcfd50f6a30338110000000.pdf Advances in Nursing Science. Vol. 30, No. 3, pp. E61–E72, 2007, Theresa Wiseman

trying to empathize, says, "Oh, that's bad news indeed, but you'll see, it will all turn out all right eventually. And hey, you did the best you could, right? You can't blame yourself for anything. So did you see the invitation we got from the Millers? Want to go this weekend? It looks like fun, and it will take your mind off of all of this."

Is this empathy?

No, it is not. Far from it! But I'm sure our well-meaning husband here is convinced he's empathetic and deserves the hubby of the year award. However, he's missing out on *all* of the four pillars. He's trying to cheer up his wife by dismissing her issue. That is not empathy, and if empathy is an important love pond to her, she will have to sit there, alone, in the dark puddle of negative emotions she's surrounded by. All she needed was some *recognition* whereas *he* came up with his manly toolbox called *solutions* that few women are ever in need of. That's why some say Google must be male and not female; before you've finished your sentence it's already coming up with multiple suggestions....

Kidding aside, what would true empathy be in this case?

"Are you serious? I'm so sorry to hear that. I know how important your clients are to you and how hard you try to help them every day. You must feel really bad. How did it happen? Do you want to talk about it? I want you to know that I'm here for you."

That is empathy. There is no judgment: "Oh well, it isn't *that* bad, now is it?" It doesn't minimize: "What are you worrying about? Didn't you watch the news? A cruise liner disappeared in the middle of the Atlantic Ocean in shark-infested waters. Seen the movie *Jaws* about that great white shark by any chance? And *Titanic*? Imagine a combination of those two! Now *that's* bad news." It is not trying to make it seem insignificant in an effort to take the pain away. *Empathy is never about taking the pain away* or trying to cheer someone up! Empathy is about showing we understand it must hurt. It's about making the connection. That's how someone with this important love pond will feel loved.

Have you ever had a conversation with someone and even though he or she was nodding along, you could feel that person wasn't really listening? That too drains this pond because the connection is lost. When a guy plants himself on the couch at night and turns on the TV even though his girlfriend is still talking to him, he just lost the connection with her. If he takes her out to a restaurant, gives the well-timed occasional nod but keeps checking his phone during the conversation, it's over. He's no longer there, and chances are the girl will start to feel unloved if situations like these happen often. There's no empathy.

Now back to Janice and Eric. I asked Janice and Eric about their goldfish because I knew their fight would very soon turn into a nice blame fest. It's like a tennis match where blames are smashed from one side to the other. Nobody will win here. As soon as eye-rolling starts (a major sign of contempt), the relationship's demise has started. And we can't really *only* hold Eric responsible. Janice attacked him after all by stating he was never there for her while he *was* already putting in a major effort (just not in the area she needed it the most).

Nevertheless, had Eric known about the love ponds and the fact that the emotional empathy one was so important to Janice, he could have stopped the argument right away by saying: "Honey, I'd love to understand why you feel that way. Tell me, what is it that you need from me that I'm not giving you because I feel like I'm doing the best I can. I must be overlooking something, so help me understand." This is Eric trying to join her in the emotional circle she found herself in. He's not defensive or argumentative. He's simply searching for a signal because he wants to connect to her. This very sentence would have been the path to the empathy and connection she desired so much. It was his willingness to see everything from her perspective, to understand her, to enter her circle, and to do so without judgment. That, in its own, is a token of love.

So many discussions and fights could end right away if we would try to see the issue from the other person's side while removing our own feelings from the equation. That's easier said than done. Our ego will often say, "No, I'm right, and the other one is wrong! My lover is hurting me so it is clear the intentions *must* be bad." But we can never blindly trust our ego or our emotions.

If emotional empathy happens to be an important love pond to you, then you'll need to communicate it very clearly to your partner by showing some empathy yourself. An example for Janice would have been: "Honey, I know you try hard to make me happy, and I appreciate that. I see that you're doing your best. But what I need most is that you're emotionally there for me. When I want to talk about something, I would love to just talk. You don't need to make me feel better; you don't need to come up with a solution. Just let me talk and try to understand what I'm feeling or what I'm going through, try to be there for me in that moment."

Eric's surprise was pretty big when I explained this concept and how empathy *really* worked. He said, "So if we never went on a vacation, if I did less around the house, if I didn't buy flowers, but instead I took the time to listen, to understand your feelings, to just be there for you... that would make you happy and feel loved?"

"Yes, baby," Janice confirmed.

Eric looked like a kid who was just told Santa wasn't real. His brain was attempting to allocate resources to grasping this strange new world that was unfolding before his eyes. For years he had put so much energy and money in things that didn't really move the love meter. All he had to do was empathize and listen, both of which cost a lot less money and time. But perhaps most importantly to Eric, his girlfriend would be happy. She would stop complaining about him and be able to give *him* much more respect, love, and affection and fill his own love ponds much more effectively. He would feel so much better in return. This is always a two-way street.

And that's exactly what happened when I followed up with them a while later. This very simple shift removed the hostility that had been brewing between them for quite some time, given that this empathy pond was a very sensitive one for Janice. This then brought out disrespectful behavior from her (not being appreciative for everything Eric did) while respect happened to be a very important pond to him. It's that vicious cycle again.

No Judging

True empathy comes without judgment. And that's more difficult than it sounds. Think of these very common conversations:

Situation: "I had a little accident with the car and destroyed the bumper. I'm so sorry!"

Reaction: "I told you to not go out in that weather!"
(Trying to prove we're smarter and/or psychic instead of understanding.)

Situation: "My boss was really unfriendly today."
Reaction: "I'm sure you're just imagining it. I've met her, and she seems a sweet woman. I'm sure it isn't that bad!" (Taking the side of the horrible boss instead of listening and trying to understand.)

Situation: "I'm coming down with the flu, and I have an important day at work tomorrow."
Reaction: "Well, at least you didn't break a leg. That would take you out for weeks." (Empathy never starts with "well, at least" and never tries to downplay the issue.)

It's not up to us to criticize, judge, or minimize. That doesn't help anyone in this case *even* if we believe they have brought it upon themselves... even if we are convinced they are making a lot of fuss about nothing.

When they consider it big and we minimize in an effort to help, we're distancing ourselves from them instead of joining them in their circle. The connection and the signal will be lost. We're there to be supportive—not to judge and punish. We always need to be on the same team *regardless of what happened*. We don't have to agree, we can have a different opinion, but they need to feel understood. Here too it's the bond and the friendship that count.

When a member of the team is in trouble, *those* troubles become the first priority of everyone. I always like to imagine two soldiers walking through a terrorist-infested city on a warm afternoon. All of a sudden shots are fired, and one soldier gets shot in the leg. Blood starts gushing out of his wound, and the soldier falls down. The other soldier, still feeling fine and in good health, says:

"Oh, well at least you didn't get run over by a tank. That would be much worse!"

or

"Say, if we make it back to camp tonight, fancy some Chinese take-out? I'm starving, and I'm sure you'll be hungry too!"

or

"Oh, it's easy! Just aim at the terrorist that shot you, and fire back! You have at least a couple of minutes before you'll lose consciousness. Don't worry! I believe in you. Good luck!"

Would any of that be helpful or in any way beneficial to the wounded soldier? Of course not! Yet, in so many relationships the hurt partner comes home, shot down, only to be welcomed with variations of these.

No. When a member of the team is shot or hurt, all else stops until that member feels taken care of. If they shoot your team member, handle it just as decisively and purposefully as if you're the one who's been shot.

That's what a true team does. That's what true friends would do, so that's definitely what true romantic partners should do (on both sides).

Sharing the Joy

Luckily, emotional empathy is not just about sharing the hardship, but the joy as well—the good and the bad. Picture a man coming home from work. He's visibly excited. He walks in the door, drops his laptop bag on the table, rushes to his wife, and kisses her on the neck. "I've given a great presentation! And you should have seen my boss. She was really happy!" says the man proudly.

"Great, great. I'm happy for you, David. Did you bring home some milk from the store?" asks the wife.

Now, David may or more probably may not have brought home some milk... and that could be a reason to point out how he always forgets everything, how he *never* helps out... but there is a time and a place for that. This is not one of them.

The wife in this example forgets to share the joy. She's not empathetic either. David had an important achievement at work and all she seems to care about is the milk. She remains at a distance and doesn't connect with him. She doesn't enter his circle of happiness and shoves his emotions off the table with a quick: "I'm happy for you. Now on to more important things. Where's the milk?"

Empathy, as we've seen, is about understanding what's important to the one we love *and showing/proving that we understand while acknowledging the emotion they feel.* Even though we may believe the milk actually *is* more important because the dinner we're preparing can't live without it.

Here's another great example of emotional empathy in action. "Honey, I know how much you love the opera. I *also* know how much I'm not fond of it. But I bought us tickets for Saturday's show. Because what I *am* fond of is seeing how happy it makes you!"

This example in particular entails a couple of important elements. It's not "I bought tickets so you can take a friend and enjoy the show. I know how much you'll love it." Empathy is about entering the other's circle and making a connection, even though we may not like it in there. It's a gift!

Love, as you're undoubtedly starting to discover, is about giving gifts. I know respect is very important to you, so I will gladly give you my respect. I understand ___ is important to you, so I will join you. I see you're feeling ____, and I'm joining you. I'm here for you, and I want to share this moment with you (good or bad!).

We give love as a gift. Love is not just something we feel; it's what we do. I love you, so I'm going to listen to what happened during your day. I'm going to listen to what made you so happy or sad, even though I have seemingly more important things to do myself. But I'm also going to spend time with you while partaking in something that is important to you. That too is about empathy.

That's how you fill this particular love pond: By emotionally being there for the other person, especially when their emotions (both good or bad) are heightened. Indeed, I always suggest the height of emotions as a guideline. Look for the heightened emotions and when you sense them, join your lover in their circle and make the connection. We can't continuously live in their circle; we have our own circles and lives too. But when emotions are high, when they need us the most, we jump in, *especially* when this proves to be an important love pond to our lover.

It's always better to take fifteen minutes a day to listen empathetically and be fully present than providing our lover one hour of semi-attentive presence that would actually *empty* this pond instead of filling it.

The Fourth Love Pond

This is one of the trickier ponds. Problems with this love pond in particular arise in many different ways. I'll share the story of Chloe and James, a couple I once met during a wedding, to illustrate. They had heard of what I do from mutual friends and couldn't wait to come over and talk to me. James and Chloe seemed like a happy couple at first glance, but James's frustration was pretty apparent.

"Brian, I thought we lived in a world where men and women were equals," James began stoically. "I love Chloe, and I think I can say she loves me too, but I feel like I'm carrying all the weight on my shoulders alone." Chloe rolled her eyes, as if she wanted to say, "There he goes again." She interrupted her man and said, "James, I do help out a lot. I go to work every day, and I pay for my half of the groceries and other bills, don't I?"

I knew this promised to be another interesting sparring contest and let it play out for a moment, even though I was thinking, "So this is really happening at a wedding of all places?" My attendance at weddings had clearly not been a good match yet.

"Yes, indeed you do," James continued. "But it's not enough. I always have to go get those groceries. I am the one doing most of the cooking. I make sure the fridge is stocked—that what needs to get replaced is replaced. I'm saving money so we can expand our house. I take care of the garden. I empty the dishwasher *way* more often than you do. I always ask to put out the lights when you've left a room, but you leave them on time and time again... need I go on?"

Chloe came back with a double-punch by stating, "Well, all of that is important to you. I wouldn't mind if we were out of toilet paper or if the electricity bill was a bit higher. I'm also not a control freak like you are. I live life day by day, and I do offer to help out, but then you always prefer to do it yourself... as if that way it would get done better." James now grimaced like a goat that accidentally started chewing a wasp. He was not at all amused.

"Yeah," James admitted, preparing his comeback as well as he could. "That's true, because when you *do* have to help out, you're always complaining afterward. I'd rather do it myself then, even though I feel like I do *everything* in and around the house. I'm trying to build something here! I want us to move forward!"

"And I don't?"

"So... do you guys have any goldfish?" I interjected.

I thought it was time for my classic pattern-interrupt. This couple was in trouble, in serious trouble. Love is... *not what we just witnessed here*. If this continued, they would soon start to resent each other and might start to look elsewhere for someone to continue their lives with. It was time to put an end to their hostility. Here too Chloe and James still had to learn that it's so much better to attack the problem instead of each other.

There were three problems. Chloe and James had different priorities in life, they were not working together as a team, and for some reason, Chloe was unwilling to give James what he needed. Whenever you hear discussions like these, some love ponds are as empty and dried out as the Mojave Desert in the middle of the summer.

When someone is not willing to give us what we need even though they easily could, we assume they *choose* not to love us. We believe they *deliberately* withhold what's important to us. If that's the person we are in a relationship with, then this is a Defcon-1 problem. It will hurt and feel like a rejection from the one we love and do so much for. So I needed to figure out why Chloe positioned her own interests and desires above those of James and most importantly, those of their relationship together. I figured it was probably because she felt James was doing the same.

"So, Chloe," I said. "It's clear what James is having trouble with, what about you? Is there anything you want from him that you're not getting?"

"Well, I miss hanging out with him. When we just started dating, he learned that I love nature and that long walks in the wild make me happy. So that's what we did every other weekend. We went to national parks or even just for a long walk in the woods close to our home. And during those walks, we could talk for hours. We never do that anymore! I still have fun by myself, and I sometimes go hiking with my girlfriends, but it's not the same. It feels like all I do is work, finish my to-do lists, and then come home to talk about the other to-dos we have in our household. And I understand they should get done, but I want to have some fun as well. Life is short, you know?"

The picture was starting to get clearer. The love ponds were emerging.

Chloe was talking about two of our previous ponds: fun and emotional empathy. Long walks in nature made her feel safe, happy, balanced. But she wanted to share that with James; she wanted him to join her in that circle of calm and all else she was feeling during those walks. But James, on the other hand, believed there wasn't time for any of that. They had a household to run, fires to put out, something to build together, and he was doing it all on his own. He had no time to enter her happy circle. It also became clear why Chloe got grumpy every time she did have to help out by shopping for groceries and performing other chores. As she was using her free time to do something she disliked; she missed the walks in nature with James *even more.* He wasn't giving her any of that either. Those are the perfect ingredients for resentment to grow.

We may consider this childish or weird, but it isn't. Our preferences and what makes us tick are personal and unique to us. And like I've been saying from the beginning of the book, if the love ponds are not filled up, unhappy, inconsiderate, withdrawn, nagging, or grumpy behavior will follow. It always does.

So I asked:

"Am I correct in presupposing that if James would take you out on those walks in nature again, if he would spend time with you doing what makes you feel alive and loved, would that motivate you to help him out in and around the house? Would you support him more in what he's trying to build?"

"Yeah sure!" Chloe confirmed. "But why is that so important?"

"Because, Chloe, what those walks in nature are to you is what nest-building is to James." And there you have it, the fourth love pond: nest-building and taking care of that nest.

Nest-builders have a couple of interesting character traits. While they often don't possess all of them, most builders love life to be predictable. They love routines and are very allergic to the unknown. Nest-builders generally tend to be more serious than playful. They want to build something and move ahead. Treading water makes them nervous and agitated. It's the story of the ants versus the cricket. The ants work hard all summer to prepare for winter. They "fear" what comes and prepare for it. The cricket has fun all day and sunbathes when he wants; he fears nothing. But when winter comes... nest-builders think ahead like the ants.

Nest-builders strongly dislike plans that change (or not having a plan at all, which, to them, feels about as comfortable as flossing the teeth of an angry rattlesnake). They usually like to have everything under control as much as they can. It reassures them and gives them stability. The keywords to remember are growth, predictability, and stability.

Given that our hectic life can be controlled just as easily as you can correctly guess the winning lottery numbers two times in a row, a lot of nest-builders love to regulate the one little part of the world they *can* potentially have under control: the home. It will be the sanctuary for some nest-builders.

If you remember Bryce and Marissa from the first love pond, nest-building was Marissa's most important love pond as well. She started to show very disrespectful behavior toward Bryce because he forgot to help out with her nest-building activities at home. That made her feel unloved.

Nest-building is a deep-seated need in most animals, and some humans have very strong nesting instincts as well. Not so much for people like Chloe who would be just as happy as a nomad or a drifter without a fixed place to live or any plans to advance in life. Chloe needs novelty and fun much more than she needs a secure nest. But to James, the stability the nest brought was vital. And the fact that his girlfriend didn't support him in building that nest was eating away at him and their relationship along with it.

Nest-builders are often cautious and are looking for security. They want a house or an apartment that can be their sanctuary; some of them want to keep it clean and well organized and are very orderly. Most nest-builders want to save money for the future or earn more money so they can get an even better nest someday or at least be ready for problems that may arrive. And they, of course, appreciate getting help. They don't want to have to repeat a request to please fix the lamp in the basement or stop wasting money on items we really don't need. They may want assistance when it comes to everything that's related to the nest. The nest is their only sanctuary, the place that is supposed to bring them safety and calm in this hectic and unpredictable world. You can imagine how frustrating it can be when another insider, someone who is living in the same nest, decides to tear it apart. *Even* if it is just a little by leaving wet towels on the floor or by failing to return the scissors to *where they belong*. Nest-builders like rules, so if someone has promised to take care of something and then doesn't, the nest-builders' love pond will start aching in frustration. If, on the other hand, others keep their promises, help out, and create predictability and safety, the nest-builder will feel loved.

How nest-building manifests itself can be very different from one nest-builder to the next, given that it's not always related to the actual home. Certain nest-builders don't want to just build a home; they're creating an empire instead and always want more. For some, nest-building is all about financial security. For them *working hard* is what nest-building is all about. They just want a nicely filled bank account and the home may not be that important. A lot of achievers are nest-builders. They want to rise to the top and build an empire for a variety of reasons, but it will often be because of some type of insecurity they drag along in their backpacks. Achieving gives them reassurance. They'd love for their partner to be the person standing next to them, never in front while trying to sabotage them by throwing a monkey wrench into their plans. Others want *everything* under control as much as they can and are very perfectionistic in general. This love pond comes in many colors. But one thing always matters: nest-builders want help and when they get hindered or when their partner doesn't *get* their nest-building needs (in whatever form they come) or holds them against them, they feel unloved.

I'll leave the psychological reasons out of this book as much as possible, but some of the fears we had as a child (e.g., being abandoned) are still present in our adult brains. They don't rule the conscious part of our brain, but the subconscious mind still plays a huge role in our feelings. For people out of this category, the mere fact that they ask for help and then don't get it triggers an alarm deep in the subconscious mind. It makes them feel like danger is near and they are all alone. Even though that may sound absolutely ridiculous to you (if this is not an important love pond in your case), I think you can understand why. Every time the nest is put in danger or the insecurity rises, the alarms go off. Most animals and even insects are built that way. Just poke around with a twig in a bee's nest and see what happens.

I want to repeat that it's not really about the nest or the house per se. It's about what it stands for: order and control in this unpredictable world. That's why, for some, seeing a wet towel on the floor hurts their nest-building pond. Others just want to be allowed to work hard. Another group may react *as* fiercely when the supply of toilet paper ran out as if the house caught fire. They both clearly are major emergencies, of course...

Luckily, this pond is very easy to fill.

Help out; and if you promise to help out, try to keep that promise. Create some predictability, and try to stick to plans that have been made. Take care of the nest if the actual home is of importance to your nest-builder. If you feel that they want to advance in life, by remodeling the home, in their career or elsewhere, try to support and not hinder them there. Nest-builders want to build a life with you. Some of their actions may seem selfish at first glance, but they're doing it for you too.

I said in one of the first chapters that happy couples consider their relationship to be a fortress, a sanctuary. Nest-builders take that literally. A woman or a man who works hard to provide for her or his family and loves doing so is a nice example. They don't appreciate it when this behavior is held against them, or when they arrive home to a messy nest. Think of Jess and Sam from the fun love pond. Jess was a nest-builder who worked hard and clearly desired their home to be clean after a long day of stressful work. As soon as she arrived home and saw the mess her cowboy had made, she felt unstable and that's when the safety that the relationship is supposed to bring starts to suffer.

Nest-building comes in many forms, but the good news is that nest-builders will often communicate *very clearly* what they need from you. If you're with a nest-builder, you won't have to guess; these will come as clear, and at first loving, requests.

- "Can you cook dinner tonight? I want to work late because I have a meeting to prepare for."
- "Can you please turn off the lights in the bathroom when you're done? I've noticed they are often on when nobody's around."
- "I'd like us to keep the bathroom and the kitchen clean. We've spent a lot of money remodeling them."
- "We'll have to leave at 6:15 tonight. Can you please make sure you're home on time?"
- "Can you pass by the store today and buy some milk? Please don't forget it, I need it for dinner."
- "Would you mind putting the scissors back in the right drawer when you're done with them?"
- "I know you say I work too much, but it's important to me. Please allow me to work hard. It's who I am and I'm doing it for us."
- "Don't forget to open a window in the bathroom after taking a shower. I don't want any mold."

Can you feel how nest-builders try to have life under control with these questions? When you help out with these requests and don't hinder them, these are all open worry loops they can now close. You're making life (and living it) so much easier for them. Mind you, these are loving requests, not orders.

"You *never* turn off the lights. You clearly have no idea how hard I have to work to pay the bills, do you?" is not a loving request. It's manipulative and meant to shove some guilt onto the other person. Nevertheless, a nest-builder may turn to this type of communication when the love pond has dried out. They will probably have asked nicely first.

Words matter, of course. If you're a nest-builder, make sure your requests are always kind and never seen as nagging or criticism. Generalizations like "you never," "why don't you ever," and "you no longer" rarely work well. They won't get you what you need. Plus, what good does it do when your lover complies for the sole reason of getting the nagging to stop? It's much more fun when it's done as an act of love.

To summarize, nest-building is about feeling in control, gaining predictability, and for some, it's about advancing. This can be achieved by helping out in and around the house, but it reaches much further than the actual home. It's everything related to living a clean, orderly, safe, secure, predictable, and protected life and doing this as a team while not being hindered by the partner in achieving this.

The Fifth Love Pond

Let's dive right in with a couple of rhetorical questions to learn more about this love pond.

Say you're at a party and you stay in the *immediate* vicinity of a person you don't really know that well. Wherever that person goes, you go. You keep that individual in sight at all times and make sure that person knows you're near. How long before "your target" starts to feel uncomfortable?

If you're going out for lunch and you're walking to your favorite restaurant with one of your colleagues, how would that colleague respond if you grabbed his or her hand, just to hold it as you both walked?

Or when returning to work after a one-week holiday, what if you hugged a colleague and instead of giving that colleague a 1-2 second friendly hug, you held on for a full 20 seconds and rested your head on your colleague's shoulders while loudly inhaling that colleague's luscious scent?

If those people didn't have a secret crush on you and didn't already have a picture of you hanging above their beds, chances are your behavior will be seen as inappropriate, very inappropriate. You've crossed a boundary that is only supposed to be crossed between people who mutually love each other. There are major cultural differences, but in general, we're supposed to remain at a certain distance from people we're not in a relationship with. When you *do* enter their personal space, they start to feel very uncomfortable. When there's a lot of love involved, however, closeness becomes somewhat the norm.

Physical closeness is indeed an important sign of love, and it is our fifth love pond. This goes from the physical act of love (making love, in other words) to staying in each other's proximity when you've been invited to your lover's Christmas party at work, to even just being together without talking or physical contact.

Some people feel loved while walking hand-in-hand and deeply need that connection; others need some space in order to not feel physically trapped. Some people can cuddle and caress for an hour. As soon as the cuddling starts, time stops. Others love a cuddle every now and then, but after a couple of seconds their efforts to remove themselves from the death grip they believe themselves to be in will increase rapidly.

Another group, mostly men, *loves* being near their lover *without talking*. A lot of men find it important to partake in certain activities with their girlfriend in silence. Some women will consider this rather strange, given that something is missing (the talking and the sharing). They may not get how their presence could possibly matter if it is to be as a silent spectator. Yet most men feel a strong connection to their girlfriend during these silent moments of just *being* together. A lot of women have had their guy ask to watch a movie together. Yet when these women dare to ask a question, "shhhh I'm watching" usually follows. This odd behavior belongs to this love pond. As strange of a phenomenon as this may seem, the presence of these women really does matter a lot.

All of these examples are related to the filling or emptying of this physical closeness love pond.

Physical closeness can be a great sign of love and connection. Imagine how loved a woman could feel if she comes home from work at night, with her boyfriend preparing dinner in the kitchen. As he sees she's upset about something, he turns off the stove, walks over to her, sits next to her, and holds her close while asking, "How was your day, honey?" If this is an important love pond for her, she'll start to feel better and will feel safe and supported almost instantly. If he then doesn't forget to *listen*, her emotional empathy pond will get a nice refill in the process.

Some people, however, prefer to have space, even within a loving relationship. This then is an important love pond to them as well. They are not hand-holders or cuddlers. Clingy behavior has the opposite effect on their physical closeness love pond and would, in fact, empty it rapidly. The good news is that it's not hard to miss this. Most people know whether their lovers like or dislike physical closeness.

Interestingly, for people who consider physical distance (instead of closeness) important, you can fill up their love pond exactly by granting them that distance and freedom. I once had a girlfriend who always wanted to sit right next to me on the couch as we were watching TV, with her legs on top of mine or with her head in my lap *all the time*. "Constant contact" was her nickname. In my personal case, this emptied this love pond quickly and made me feel like I was constantly being hugged by a boa constrictor. Even though I love a short cuddle, her lengthy entrapments were an oppressive feeling that I could not enjoy.

As a consequence, this love pond emptied rapidly and changed my behavior toward her: I became very distant and *needed space. Not* just on the couch. As we've seen, when one of the love ponds gets empty you can expect some unwarranted and irrational behavior from your lover. Her granting me some physical freedom and alone time was what kept this particular love pond all filled up in our case. Furthermore, thanks to that distance I felt much more attracted to her and started to cuddle *her* more, started holding her hand, and so forth on my own initiative. Because she had created that distance, now I wanted to bridge that gap. Our minds work in funny and often childish ways. This is another prime example of how taking care of the needs of your lover can give you more genuine love in return.

Evidently, this is one of the love ponds where it would *really* come in handy if both parties of the couple happen to give the same importance to it. But there is no serious problem when this isn't the case. The act of love comes from the choice of being willing to fill up the love pond of the one you love.

Let's look at Hugo. Hugo is a guy who really needs his space. Handholding is for children, cuddling for teddy bears, and caressing is for everyone who's not named Hugo. Hugo needs his alone time too. He can't spend more than an hour with his girlfriend or he gets jerky and needs to go "do" something. But last week, Rhonda, his long-term girlfriend, needed him. Her father was lying in a coma in the hospital. She was an only child, and her mother had passed a long time ago. Rhonda wanted to spend as much time in the hospital as she could, holding her father's hand. Physical closeness was indeed very important to her. This time, however, Hugo knew his girlfriend really needed him. He took time off from work and spent *every free minute* he had by her side, sitting right next to her. This was a huge effort for him, considering his need for space, but he loved Rhonda and wanted her to feel supported. Even though Rhonda was too sad and scared to really acknowledge how much it meant to her, she later thought it was the sweetest thing Hugo had ever done. Had he been absent, she might have felt so alone that she would have never forgotten it.

Hugo and Rhonda balance this love pond perfectly. It's an important one to both of them (Hugo needs space and alone time, Rhonda needs closeness), and they each know very well when to give space and when to provide closeness. Love is a choice.

The Many Types of Physical Closeness

The physical closeness pond affects relationships in many ways. First, sexual activity is crucial in every relationship. It's what distinguishes lovers from people who are just friends. If you're in a long-term monogamous relationship, both of you will be fully and exclusively responsible for each other's sexual pleasure. It's quite the task when you think of it.

Nevertheless, "having sex" has nothing to do with this particular love pond. Sex has to be present, regardless of the importance of this specific love pond. It's not because a man needs to have sex that this love pond is important to him. That's physical closeness on another level. He may love sex (and he will) but feel indifferent to holding hands or sitting too close together, for instance.

Making love, however, *is* related to this love pond. Making love is different than just having sex. To make it stereotypical, it's the man taking the time to light some candles, to put on some soft music, to turn up the heat, and to give his woman a good foot massage. Then he goes to her shoulders, slowly undresses her, and massages her back. Only after some extensive foreplay does he go for the actual physical act of sex. But even the sex is different. There's a lot of caressing, light and soft kisses. It's clear that it's not just about his mechanical sexual pleasure but making his woman feel safe, loved, and taken care of. This means that mere seconds after sex, he won't just roll over and snooze. Instead, he will still be attending and caring for her while fighting the urge to doze off.

There's an easy-to-miss level to this sexual part as well. Some people want to *merge or fuse* with their lover by having deep conversations while opening up fully. Others can only feel *that* close through making love. Strange as that may sound to some, becoming one helps them connect on an *emotional* level, even though the act itself is physical. In this case, making love and feeling desired by their lover brings them the safety, the validation, and the acceptance they are longing for. Indeed, both the emotional empathy pond we saw earlier and this physical pond here are a possible source of *emotional* connection.

Another form of physical closeness is spending time together. That could be going for long walks while holding hands, or joining your significant other during family or friend visits (especially when you'd rather take a stroll on the North Pole than see *those* people).

And as mentioned before, actual physical contact may not be required. During my interviews, I met many couples who loved being together without talking or touching. Examples are watching a movie together, the woman who's writing a blog post while her boyfriend is reading the paper at the same table, sitting somewhere in nature side by side while enjoying the view. This pond is about everything that involves being physically close. It's the purest way to communicate, "We're in this together, and I'm part of your team. I'm here for you. *Right* here."

Even though this pond is not a *sensitive* one for most people, it always matters. It's worth taking the time to find out what our partner's physical closeness needs look like and making sure this pond is well looked after. This is the pond that makes the difference between being "brother and sister," colleagues, or just friends, and being in a loving, passionate relationship.

The Sixth Love Pond

I'll get straight to the point for this one. The sixth love pond is the "I thought of you" pond. This is a very interesting and challenging one because it has some important pitfalls.

Think of Jesse, who arrives a couple of minutes late at the restaurant where he's meeting his girlfriend for lunch. He had warned her that his meeting might run a bit late, so Monica had already asked for their preferred table and had ordered his favorite vegetable juice along with gluten-free lasagna, something he is fond of as well. He normally drinks a glass of red wine, but Monica skipped that considering he had informed her about a presentation he has to give in the afternoon. She knows wine can make him sleepy, so she ordered the brand of sparkling water her boyfriend loves. When Jesse arrives, he's so pleased to see his girlfriend thought of what is important to him. She hadn't even forgotten about that big presentation, even though he had mentioned it only once over a week ago. He feels very loved at that moment. As you can see, this too is a strong sign of "I know you, I understand what's important to you, and I thought of you."

There are many examples for this pond. "Can you please pick up some milk before returning home tomorrow night?" and then not forgetting about it is another one. This particular example can belong both to the nest-building pond (keeping a promise creates predictability and closes a worry-loop of the nest-builder) *and* this one (the not forgetting about it). When we complete tasks like these, we prove that we have been thinking of our lover, that we are a team, and that we are willing to put in the effort for them. We're also willing to spend time supporting what's valuable to them, even though it may require an effort.

Interestingly, this is one of the only love ponds you can fill without being physically present. Think of the guy who sends a picture of a cute dog he saw in the park to his girlfriend. It's the dog breed she's so fond of. This, again, is a sign that he's thinking about her *and that he deliberately chose this action to make her feel good*. She's clearly on his mind and if this love pond is important to her, it will make her feel loved. A guy who picks out a well-thought-out gift for his girlfriend's birthday and hands it to her will fill up this love pond. Not because of the gift, but because of what it stands for: I thought this through, you are important to me, and I put in an effort to make you feel loved.

I'm sure you can sense how easy it is to flash-empty this pond. Great ways to make someone feel unloved are indeed forgetting important dates or events, forgetting about conversations we've had with our lover, *not* bringing home the milk even though it was asked for, *not* removing wet towels from the floor even though it was kindly requested... 73 times before. In short, by not remembering something that was clearly communicated as essential or by otherwise proving we're unwilling to put in an effort, we hurt this love pond.

Imagine the feeling one of my clients had as she was giving a presentation for her newly launched book, only to feel discouraged because she couldn't spot her husband amongst the crowd. He forgot to show up, even though he had promised to be there and should have known how important this day was to his wife. He wasn't physically present and thus emptied her physical closeness pond. He wasn't sharing the joy, and thus emptied her emotional empathy pond. He forgot about this "I thought of you and what's important to you becomes important to me" pond *and* all of this was obviously very inconsiderate too. There was little he could have done to make her feel more unloved that night.

Nobody has heard of him ever since.

I'm kidding. He made up for it.

Every "I thought of you" signal is very loving because our mind favors to think about what's valuable to us and tends to forget what is insignificant. When someone is on our mind a lot, they're obviously important to us. When we put in an effort and not only think about them, but complete a to-do for the sole purpose of making the other person feel good and loved, we fill up this love pond. It's a pure sign of love.

This is a pretty easy love pond to understand and to fill: perform actions that say "I thought of you." Be considerate. Spend time proving that you thought of your lover. Here, as you undoubtedly see, words and promises don't matter. Only actions count. Even though this one is easy to fill, the challenge, however, is that it's also effortless to empty it. For some reason that I won't try to make excuses for, men have a tougher time filling this pond than most women. A man is perfectly capable of loving his wife dearly and *still* forgetting all about their wedding anniversary... especially if his wife didn't remind him. You've probably heard that if a woman wants to scare her husband, *all* she has to do is ask him if he remembers what today is...

An Important Word of Caution

This pond obviously matters to most people. Nonetheless, it can easily be overdone and will then have an opposite and detrimental effect. Think of a sweet woman—the typical nice girl—who's been with her boyfriend for less than three months. One day she arrives at his apartment with a gift. Not just any gift: it's the first, *signed* edition of a book his father used to read bedtime stories from while he was a child, something he just mentioned in passing. She went to great lengths to get this book—that much is obvious. His reaction startles her, as he says, "Oh thank you. You really shouldn't have." It may seem like our guy here is ungrateful. He's not. This was only one of the many times she overdid it during her *make him feel good and loved* mission. Last week she had bought him new underwear as a gift. On Sunday she decided to make him a four-course dinner to show off her cooking skills. She texts him sweet notes at least twice *every* day. Did I mention she only listens to music *he* likes when they are in her car and that she tries to satisfy his every whim whenever they are together? Even whims he doesn't have...

Long story short: she's proving daily that she thinks about him non-stop. He's clearly the *only* thing on her mind. I repeat they had only been seeing each other for about three months. Aside from the timing, this is just too much at any point in the relationship. She really shouldn't have indeed. I like to call this concept the hot fudge sundae effect. Most people like to eat ice cream. But when they get served the entire bucket at once, stomachaches follow swiftly. We have to spoon-feed this love pond and go slow. Overcompensating is a word that's not found in the dictionary of love.

This is a true story, sadly. It's pretty clear our nice girl here was very insecure. All of her gestures were requests for validation, for proof that he still liked her. She was trying to *buy* his love and attention. Although she believed otherwise at first, these actions were not *real* tokens of love; they were tokens of insecurity and weakness. She was just searching for reassurance. She was trying to prove herself to him. In doing so, she lowered her own value and drove him away. True, mature love always has a basis of strength, never of weakness or neediness, as we've already covered.

I've seen many men and women make this mistake over the years (I myself was also a proud member of this club until my late-twenties). We should of course give and invest into the relationship, but never overdo it nor lose our integrity and above all, never give in order to get something in return.

The Seventh Love Pond

The final pond doesn't matter to a lot of people, that's why it's last. Yet, for those who do find it important, it can be an absolute deal breaker; these people have a hard time surviving when this pond is not filled. The seventh pond is what I call the organizing and coaching love pond, aka the "being the mother" pond. You'll never hear people for whom this love pond is important say, "I can take care of that myself, thank you very much!" They love to get support and be helped out. Sometimes, they desperately need it.

I first found out about this love pond by looking at how successful couples deal with life, real day-to-day life. In the fifties, the traditional setting was one where the woman decided everything in the household. That was her responsibility and the man needn't worry or care about it. He didn't have to think about where or what they were going to eat for dinner, what present to bring to the Jones' barbeque next weekend, or what to pack when they were going away on holiday. She took care of it—all of it. She, as the mother, organized *everything* and was clearly in the lead. Had you asked her what color of socks her husband was wearing on any given day, she'd probably know the answer.

Times have, thankfully, changed, and this role is no longer tied to a specific gender, but it's still an issue for some. You'll surely know men who really *do* still need a "mother" who thinks of everything. And the fact that their girlfriend or wife is willing to take on that task makes them feel deeply loved. You'll find women who don't want to worry about the organization and feel loved when their boyfriend takes care of it. I once was with a girl who virtually *couldn't* organize anything. If it were up to her, we would have continuously ran out of toilet paper, bottled water, and food and, our electricity would have been cut plenty of times for bills that weren't paid on time. Claiming that she was forgetful was an understatement. The fact that I took the organization of the household on myself was a nice token of love to her. She obviously helped with the execution.

This pond is different from the nest-building pond because it has nothing to do with seeking security or the nest itself. This pond is not about achieving, building something together, helping out around the house, and performing the actual tasks. It's about taking the lead in the *organization* of everything; it's about being the good old-fashioned "mother" or director. It's purely practical and about taking on some (or all) of the responsibilities. The actual helping out should always be shared equally.

When a man with organizing and coaching as his most sensitive love pond is on holiday with his girlfriend, he'll follow *her* lead as to when they need to get a cab to the airport. In the airport, he'll carry most of the luggage—that she probably packed—but will leave it up to her to find the right gate, to choose where to sit, etc. He loves it when she takes care of it, and it makes him feel loved when she doesn't mind organizing it all.

So, for this love pond, try to figure out where both you and your partner stand. Who needs "mothering" with what? Then try to find the equilibrium you can both be happy with. In relationships where this pond is at the bottom of the list for both parties, responsibilities are shared equally. The need for mothering will be non-existent. In couples where this pond does play a major role, one of them will clearly be in the practical lead.

**

We've now gone over the seven important love ponds. Most of the love ponds will matter to everyone, but the point will now be to figure out the sensitivity and the status of the love ponds. Remember that in great relationships, both partners do what's required so both can feel loved most of the time. Both people should fill up the love ponds when needed and empty them as little as possible.

In the next chapters, we'll find out how to make the love flow well within the relationship and what mistakes we should all avoid for the relationship to last as long as possible.

To recap, the seven ponds are:

> Respect: due regard for the feelings and wishes of our lover plus the careful handling of sensitive egos. Making our lover feel valued and significant, especially when it's a sensitive pond.

> Fun and some unpredictability: keeping it light and funny every now and then and steering clear of negativity as much as possible. Bringing a positive atmosphere both to the activities *and* the communication.

> Emotional empathy: listening without judging, trying to understand, confirming that our partner's feelings make sense (even though we may not agree and communicate that as well), and being there for them on an emotional level. In other words, creating a connection with our lover.

> Nest-building: helping with protecting the nest or treating it as a sanctuary. In many cases also creating

predictability in other ways, saving and making money, working on the future together, and sticking to plans. Being the ant instead of the cricket. Making life better by supporting a career or by working on the expansion of the actual nest. Most importantly, *not* hindering the nest-builder in what the nest-building stands for in his or her case.

Physical closeness: creating a physical connection by being near our lover, not leaving them alone, holding hands, cuddling, being physically present when needed. Or, on the contrary, the exact opposite and granting space and alone-time when requested. Where emotional empathy was purely about the emotions, this pond is purely physical.

I thought of you: showing how valuable our lover is to us by proving that we've thought of them by remembering important dates, knowing what our lover likes and dislikes, remembering what was said, and so forth. In short, proving that we have our lover in mind, that we *know* them, and that we're willing to put in an effort for them.

Organizing and coaching (aka "mothering"): taking the lead when asked, taking care of the practical organization, and helping to carry some or most of the day-to-day responsibilities (not with the execution, this should always be shared equally).

You can already start to map out their importance in your and your partner's case and figure out to what extent the love ponds are currently filled. This will help you choose what to devote most of your time to. If your relationship is in trouble, look for dried-up or sensitive love ponds. You will need to investigate a little bit because, as seen, the love ponds can be filled and emptied in many ways that will be very personal to both you and your partner. We're all wired differently. You'll get help with your investigation in a later chapter.

The Key to Long-Term Passion

Now that we've covered the love ponds, let's look at how we can make sure our *own* love ponds get filled while we avoid becoming a doormat or accidently diminishing the passion in our relationship.

The key happens to be the famous sentence: "Just be yourself." It has to be the most shared sentence to anyone asking for advice regarding their love life or more specifically their dating life. It's the magic formula; when one is her or his self, all problems supposedly vanish.

I believe that to be true for the most part. Just not in the way some people understand it. It's never about feeling and then acting jealous or needy and being our own worst selves. It's the exact opposite. This misunderstanding holds one of the more important keys to the *lack of passion* some couples experience in their long-term relationships.

When two people just met and fell in love, they want to spend every second together. You can tell the difference between a couple that has just met versus a couple that has been together for a decade by watching how they behave in a restaurant. The new couple will be chattering like nervous chickens. If you walk past some long-term couples, however, you'll probably hear crickets instead. The silence may be deafening. The reason is simple. The freshly "we've recently met and are so in love" couple is still in the process of getting closer to each other. They're full of insecurities about one another, full of wonder and uncertainty. Most of their conversation is about trying to get to know the object of their attraction, trying to make sure that the happily ever after can get started a.s.a.p.

As they become closer, however, some couples fuse too much and overdo it. They are so intimate that they start to lose their sense of self. This is when doormats are born and passion quietly exits through the backdoor. Dependent or codependent relationships are rarely healthy, of course. Think of the nice girl who continuously thinks about pleasing her guy, trying to find out how she can make him happy or how she can prove she's better than other women. When he's in a bad mood, she adapts, believes it's somewhat her responsibility, and tries to cheer him up. When he withdraws, or worse, ignores her, she will figure out a strategy to change that and reel him back in. She tries to adapt to his needs and wants and in doing so, totally forgets about her own. Nice guys make the same mistake. Most of what they do is done in an effort to please their girlfriend or wife. This will often drastically reduce the passion the woman feels for them.

Instead of being themselves, these people start to make it *all* about the other person. Nothing kills passion more than continuously prioritizing the love ponds and needs of our partner over our own. It's a dead-end street.

The vital concept of being ourselves means there is enough space between both parties, *even* when they are in a committed long-term relationship.

Firstly, when we are in a relationship, we're supposed to maintain our own lives as well. There's my life, there's your life, and there is our life. These three should never *fully* merge. It's what keeps a relationship fresh in the long term; it's what generates active conversation at the dinner table, both at home *and* in restaurants. We'll have experiences to talk about. This is that crucial distance between both parties that allows them to still long for each other.

Secondly, this not only relates to physical distance. The mental part should not be underestimated because it's key. When we are able to be very close to each other and *still* manage to hold on to our own self, we can enjoy a lifetime of passion within the same relationship.

How do we hold on to our own selves? By remembering that we are a different person than our lover and by not being afraid to actually show those differences. If we want a true connection with someone, we first have to allow ourselves to be seen. We have our own needs, rights, aspirations, ideas, and beliefs, just as our partner does. They should not be hidden. What we *are* is never subordinate or superior to what our lover is. This indispensable distance is achieved by having clear boundaries and by not being afraid to point them out.

All of this has important ramifications that you will be able to reap the rewards from for decades to come. When we are not afraid to stand up for ourselves and actually *be* ourselves, we risk rejection. In some way, we are saying, "Here I am. *This* is me, and this is what I need to be happy and even though I will respect your needs, rights, beliefs, and so on, they are not more important than my own." We never hide.

Some people are scared of this concept because they fear losing their lover in the process. They would prefer to adapt in order to keep the peace and never create any friction. This, again, is how doormats are born. True doormats feel the needs of others, often including their pets, and keep putting their own needs aside to get rid of that feeling of guilt they otherwise feel. It's a feeling they cannot stand. However, when we truly are ourselves and the other person *doesn't* leave, magic happens. Now we can finally feel genuinely loved, secure, and safe. That's what real love is about; it's never about playing games. This is the only viable approach in long-term relationships.

I hope you can feel the power of this concept. If we adapt to our lover and get some attention and love in return because of it, it won't satisfy our hunger for *real, genuine* love. We'll know we *bought* it. If, however, we know our partner loves us, even though we didn't lose our integrity and didn't place our lover's needs above or beneath our own, now the love can feel real. We should fulfill our partner's desires and we often have to go first, but we can never forget about ourselves.

Being ourselves also means we can show who we are, without expecting acceptance or validation from our lover. I'll give a silly example. If I tell my girlfriend, "I hope you don't think this is strange, but, well, it's important to me that when we set a date to meet somewhere you arrive on time. You know... if you don't mind" then the fact that I am hesitantly communicating proves I'm praying for her acceptance of my boundary. I'm fearing her rejection of my need and possibly me as a person. That's weak behavior. It's not really a boundary if I'm asking her if she's OK with it. This is not an example of being myself, given that I still link my behavior up to her reaction. I'm adapting like a regular doormat. It's me being my weakest self.

If, on the other hand, I'd say, "Honey, you have every right to be late, you can do as you please. However, it's important to me that you arrive on time from now on," then I've clearly stated my need in a non-needy, non-negative, non-manipulative, non-angry, and yet very effective way. I'm communicating: *your needs and rights matter, but mine do just as much.* Will she be on time from then on? That's really up to her to decide, of course. If we have to force or manipulate someone to get our needs met, we will still feel unloved.

There's no point in ever following that approach within a romantic relationship.

We state our boundary and our needs, we show who we really are, and then we give our partner the full freedom to behave as they please. It's the only way. If they choose to not take care of what is important to us and make us feel unhappy even though we took care of their needs, we draw our conclusions and move on if needed. Chances are, however, that the indispensable distance I've just explained will feed their desire to make us happy.

That same distance created by holding on to ourselves happens to be one of the most important keys to maintaining long-term (sexual) passion within relationships. It's what cultivates the longing. This concept tackles two birds with one stone.

I admit it's not an easy equilibrium, especially when there are conflicting needs. There will be. Nevertheless, as you've seen in some of the real-life examples I've given, it's perfectly possible to find a balance where, over time, both of our efforts are equal while our needs are also met. If all of our combined love ponds are cared for, that equilibrium is there by definition. *If* on top of that we can stay away from toxic behaviors like attacks, criticism, cynicism, and contempt, the relationship will flourish. Let's explore how that's done in what follows.

How Bad Are Arguments?

As I was studying and observing successful couples, I found plenty of them who had conversations that looked like they didn't get along at all. But at the same time, you could *at all times* feel that there was sufficient love flowing between the both of them. In fact, so much love was present that they didn't have to watch their words or walk on eggshells. They could both see right through the "fighting" because they *knew* their partner loved them. And what's interesting is that both parties had to taste defeat at times.

"I wish you would have worn a different jacket."
"What's wrong with my jacket? I love it."
"Well, I *don't!*"

I was listening in on an older couple sitting at the table next to me in a fancy restaurant. It was clear the woman *really* didn't like that jacket.

"It makes me look like I matter, and I like that."
"No, it makes you look like someone who's trying too hard."
"You know I love to try hard to impress you. Don't you, Liz?"

The woman started to smile and blush a bit.

"I still don't like it," she added with a reluctant grin on her face.
"No, but you're right. I'll throw it away tonight like I've done a couple of times before. But I swear, it always finds the way back to my closet. I have absolutely positively nothing to do with that," the man said, smiling just as much as his wife. "How's your wine, my dear?"

And the conversation continued.

At first, this seemed like a pretty aggressive and feisty conversation, and it was, but there was an undertone of love and affection. Good couples *do* have arguments, fights even. They do tend to attack each other every now and then, but it doesn't matter because the undertone of respect, understanding, and emotional intelligence is always present. The fights never get childish or dirty.

This was an actual discussion I witnessed firsthand, but I'll now turn it into a disrespectful one void of love to prove my point. Here's what it would have looked like without respect or empathy but with criticism and contempt instead:

"I wish you would have worn a different jacket."
"What's wrong with my jacket? I love it."
"Well, I don't."
"Why don't you just keep your opinion to yourself?"

OR

...
"Well, I don't."
"Well, I don't like the dress you're wearing."

OR

...
"Well, I don't."
"Stop attacking me! I can wear whatever I want!"

In these hypothetical examples, the conversation becomes a power struggle. There is no team or friendship, and it's clear the important bond is severely damaged. Most of the couples

I've had to coach had many of *these* types of discussions and some were unaware of how devastating they are.

The best relationships and marriages have conflicts; some have a lot of them! Likewise, I've seen people divorce who never even had an argument. Do you remember the woman I started off this book with? The one who got married only to divorce a couple of months later? She and her fiancé/husband never had fights. Ever. We saw how well that turned out.

The secret of lasting love isn't in whether arguments, conflicts, and fights are absent. It lies in the choice of love, in the caring for each other, in the putting the team above the individual person. As I said, every happy couple will tell you they are best friends. It's the necessary element I found every time in the happy couples I interviewed.

The Secret Sauce to Lasting Love

The secret of a fulfilling life, regardless of what area of life we're focusing upon, is emotional intelligence. It's hard to apply, but when done correctly, the rewards are huge.

Famous scientific experiments like the Marshmallow Test have scientifically proven it decades ago.[5] In that experiment, young children were asked to wait all alone in a room while they were sitting at a table. One by one, the researcher had put a marshmallow in front of these kids and asked them not to eat it. They could eat it if they wanted, but if they waited, they'd get another marshmallow upon the return of the researcher. When these kids were left by themselves, the fight against their emotions began. Some kids ate the marshmallow straight away; others fought their urge—often in very amusing ways—till the very end so they could enjoy the bonus marshmallow.

That is emotional intelligence in action. Superseding a dominating emotion because we rationally know it isn't serving us. Not eating and waiting was clearly the better choice. Researchers from this study then continued to follow those kids throughout their lives for decades and found that those who were emotionally intelligent (those who waited for the return of the researcher) had significantly better lives in all areas of life, not just on the weight scale.

Unsurprisingly, research has proven that couples that are emotionally intelligent within their relationship form significantly better relationships than those who do not.[6]

[5] https://hbr.org/2014/09/the-marshmallow-test-for-grownups
[6] Emotional Intelligence and its Relationship with Marital Adjustment and Health of Spouse, Journal of Social Science Researches Vol. 7, No. 2, October, 2010, PP. 38-46, Rakesh Pandey and Tulika Anand

Apply emotional intelligence by detaching from hurtful emotions—emotions that can hurt the future of the relationship—and choose a better path that serves the relationship. It's always the path without negativity, without nagging, without criticism and cynicism, or anything else that destroys relationships. You won't be able to avoid the emotions, but you always choose how you act upon them.

All of this sounds very easy in theory and you may be nodding along as you read this, but it is hard to apply when you're the one feeling all of those emotions. Nevertheless, I have a special strategy that I hope you'll try. When we're in the midst of an argument or a power struggle, our ego is under attack. Our feelings are hurt, and it will be very hard to be kind or do what's best for the future of the relationship. Our ego just wants to set the record straight and fast!

As I was helping other couples, I noticed that, when hurt, it's easier to "do it for the relationship" than for "the partner" (given that that's the one who hurt our feelings, the one who our ego has singled out as the root cause of all evil). So this is a little trick to make using your emotional intelligence a bit easier. If you cannot get yourself to do what's best for your partner, do it for the relationship instead.

I'll give you a personal example from my own relationship. I had hurt my girlfriend's feelings, something that I, being a man, seemingly do often.

"You were rude earlier," she said.
"Um, when?"
"When I came home and you snapped at me because something was burning up in the kitchen."
"What? I wasn't rude!" I said, with my empathy engine in sleeping mode.

That's when the ping-pong battle started and the decibels of our voices started to increase. The power struggle between our egos had begun. Mine started to wish a camera had recorded what had *really* happened, so I could use it as evidence of my pure, almost angel-like goodness during this trial where I was clearly being wrongfully accused. It was quite clear I had really hurt my girlfriend's feelings, but I honestly couldn't see *how* I had done it. Something was indeed burning in the kitchen when I cut a conversation short and ran over to the stove. In my defense, I'm a nest-builder, so I was trying to get us the nutrients we needed by cooking us a great meal while preferring not to burn down the entire house. My ego was convinced I was innocent.

Nevertheless, that was not important or even relevant because my girlfriend's feelings were hurt. That was the only thing that really mattered at that moment, not the "how." My team member was in trouble; that's what counts. Albeit I failed to see it right away because my emotions were clouding my vision. I was not emotionally intelligent up until that point of our heated discussion.

As the discussion started to become a loud fight, it was clear I wasn't going to convince her of my lack of wrongdoing. Then my emotional intelligence finally kicked in, and I decided to choose the relationship over my now hurt ego. I did not do what followed for my girlfriend (my hurt ego still wouldn't let me); I did it for the relationship. I walked over to my girlfriend, picked her up as she was still yelling at me, and I said, "You can keep yelling. I understand you're upset, but I'm going to be giving you little kisses in the meantime." And, with her up in the air, I danced around a bit as I was flooding her with kisses. I really wish we had a camera....

Guess what happened? It took her three full seconds before she started to laugh. This was a major pattern interrupt. The last thing she and her ego had expected for me to do was *this*.

My girlfriend has followed a similar approach many times when I was the one who went on an irrational tantrum. This works miracles. If you can't do it for your partner in the midst of a power struggle, do it for the relationship.

There are many reasons why this technique works so well *if* there's still sufficient love present in the relationship. First of all, as I said, it's a pattern interrupt. The pattern is the increasing hostility; the interrupt is the last thing you'd expect at that time (in this case, being picked up and kissed). It snaps the other person out of whatever emotional state they were in, helping *them* to be more emotionally intelligent in return. You can choose anything you want as a pattern interrupt. It just has to be unexpected, not hostile (no chainsaws, axes, or sentences like *"release the hounds"* should be used) and totally different from what you'd normally do.

Second, it shows her that I still love her, and actions always speak louder than words. I can try to convince her I didn't mean any harm as much as I want, but she won't believe it because she's hurt. She's overrun by emotions herself. But actions speak so loud that she had no other choice than to feel my love and affection for her.

Third, it is emotional intelligence at play. We were both getting caught up in negative emotions that weren't serving the relationship and the future of it in any way. Emotional intelligence within relationships means that at least one of the parties realizes this and prevents the situation from escalating any further. One person is all it takes!

You can do this by saying, "Honey, I love you, and I'm going to leave the room for a while so we can cool down," or by making fun *of yourself*, or by doing anything else that makes the other person laugh or receive a shot of love.

I've noticed—both in the couples I've coached and studied and in my own relationships—this approach works remarkably well *if* the base of the relationship has been taken care of. Meaning that the love ponds are mostly filled and the friendship is stable. That makes this emotional intelligence approach an important barometer for the future of the relationship. When *even this* doesn't work, the relationship *is* already failing! Urgent repairs are needed, and some love ponds and the friendship are severely damaged. This is obviously a *huge* red flag.

That may sound like bad news since what good is the secret sauce if it doesn't work when the relationship is in trouble? It's the secret sauce because it is meant to *prevent* the relationship from *getting* in trouble. Downward spirals don't happen overnight; they happen when there have been too many negative discussions and emotionally unintelligent fights that leave either or both parties feeling hurt, rejected, or angry and the neighbors wondering if all that yelling was *really* necessary. That's why it's important to always apply some of the secret sauce during every fight and discussion. Don't worry. We'll deal with relationships really in trouble in a later chapter.

Let's return to the older man whose wife didn't like his jacket. Let's look at it again:

"It makes me look like I matter, and I like that."
"No, it makes you look like someone who's trying too hard."
"You know I love to try hard to impress you. Don't you, Liz?"

"I still don't like it," the woman added with a huge grin on her face.

"No, but you're right. I'll throw it away tonight like I've done a couple of times before. But I swear, it always finds the way back to my closet," the man said, smiling just as much as his wife. "How's your wine, my dear?"

Even though this was far from a fight, for some couples this would have inevitably led to one. Not for these two elderly lovers. This was an example of a pattern interrupt and emotional intelligence. The normal course of the pattern would be for him to get defensive and possibly attack her back, fighting fire with fire. But he didn't. Although she was seemingly out to get him, he acted like a friend, made a loving joke, filled up the *fun* love pond while he was at it, smiled, and then added another joke. Also, notice that he wasn't acting like a doormat either; he stood his ground *without* becoming angry or negative. All of this is proof of his integrity, their bond and existing love. Even though there was some temporary hostility coming from the lady who may have had a bad day, her man didn't respond with anger. He didn't fight fire with fire. He loved her and knew that she loved him too (probably basing this on how well she treated him and cared for his love ponds otherwise).

Discussions like these and even fights are unavoidable. Don't even try to avoid them! Learn how to deal with them in the most emotionally intelligent way possible to protect the relationship. It requires kindness and love, combined with a pattern interrupt when needed. It's really hard at first, but practice makes perfect.

I Know You

Take the time to really get to know each other, not just because your lover will feel understood but because you will be able to explain *their* behavior much better to yourself and thus prevent unnecessary hostility and worry. In other words, learn about each other's love ponds and their love status. How loved does your partner feel in each of the ponds? Are their important needs mostly met? Learn about what matters, but also learn about trigger points—things that hurt our partner even when it makes absolutely no sense to us personally.

Picture a man coming home from work. He finds his wife reading in the living room. He kisses her on the forehead and asks what's for dinner. His wife looks up angrily and says, "Is that all I'm good for? Really?"

This is one of the many pivotal moments that define the future of their relationship. It was her night to cook, so her response was totally uncalled for according to his ego. Our guy could now respond in anger by saying, "Why are you talking like that to me? I did nothing wrong! I come home after a hard day of work, and there you are attacking me! I cooked us a meal yesterday!" In other words: he can play the victim and he very well may, given that her reaction hurt his respect pond. This will lead to a fight and eventually to nothing... as in the relationship will not survive when moments like these keep repeating themselves.

Our guy could also say, "I'm sorry, honey. I'll cook." But that wouldn't be the right choice either. A good relationship is about equality, not becoming a docile slave to avoid the wrath of our lover. There's no room for doormats in great relationships.

He could instead have taken the time to *know* his wife and think, "She normally doesn't behave like this, so something's wrong." Consequently, he sits down next to his wife and says, "What's going on, baby? Did something happen at work? Do you want to talk about it?" This comes from a position of strength while responding in a loving, empathetic way. He does this because she usually treats him very well.

His wife now reluctantly opens up and says, "Karen stabbed me in the back today. She took the credit for something I did."

"I told you, you shouldn't trust her," he says, putting an immediate end to the empathy and equality. He's now talking down at her from his high horse. His wife is opening up, and he arrogantly lashes out. Not a good idea.

He could also say, "Well, just call your boss and tell her that..." But that's not a good idea either. Men coming up with solutions all the time usually doesn't end well.

Instead, our hypothetical perfect guy uses his emotional intelligence and turns on the empathy engine some more. He steps into her circle and says, "Tell me about it. What did she do?" He continues to listen *and* cooks dinner later on.

But why? She did treat him unfairly, didn't she? Why would she deserve a good treatment? We shouldn't reward her bad behavior, right?

Great partners in great relationships will—as I've repeatedly found to be true—not take things at face value. They look at more than what just happened *right now*.

In this example, the wife would normally not act like this, so our guy instinctively knows something is on her mind. Some men would then block themselves off emotionally and go fiddle with some tools in the garage, hide behind their computer screen, or at the very least go elsewhere to stick their head in the sand. They would give *everything* to avoid the emotional conversation that would undoubtedly follow. But those aren't solutions. That would only increase the emotional gap between the both of them. We're supposed to be a *team* in the relationship.

What he does is not *just* so she would feel understood. *He* wants to understand why she acted that way for himself. It's a lot harder for resentment and even contempt to build when we understand why our lover just hurt our feelings or behaved in a non-optimal way. It will often not have been personal at all, even though it absolutely, positively felt that way.

Relationships go downhill fast when we start to focus on the negative, so our guy here does the opposite. Instead of becoming defensive or hostile, he looks for the positive and asks himself, "Is my wife a bad person? Is my wife out to hurt my feelings? Is that who she is? No! She is not, so something must be going on. Let's find out what."

It sounds so simple and silly when you read it, doesn't it? Yet this is one of the hardest things to do within a relationship, especially when it's not the first time your partner has hurt your feelings. Our guy does feel hurt by her reaction; he's human and will need to use a lot of his emotional intelligence. If her reaction *really* hurt him, he can always use the "I won't do it for her, but for the relationship" strategy that we learned in the last chapter.

The more we know and understand our partner, the more we will be able to explain certain behaviors. And when we do, we can look past what just happened and more easily use our emotional intelligence. We should then wonder: "Is this a cry for help? What's going on here? What does my lover need from me? How can I help?"

Evidently, knowing what your lover wants and needs even when your partner hasn't told you is an amazing sign of love and caring that will simultaneously fill multiple love ponds.

I Like That About You

Now let's look at a great formula to get some good old resentment going and then what to do about it. This will come in handy if you ever come to the conclusion that resentment inconspicuously found its way into your precious relationship.

Our mind's natural state is to focus on the negative. It has to. If you're in the midst of the jungle enjoying all the flowers and butterflies (the positive), your mind unquestionably has to single out the two eyes of that well-hidden, hungry jaguar lurking in the background (the negative). Even when everything is beautiful, the mind *absolutely has to* filter out and then focus on the negative for the sake of our own survival. People who didn't have this filter just didn't make it. They were still admiring a butterfly when the roaring jaguar stood right next to them asking if he could have a bite to eat. He probably didn't take "no" for an answer, so this ignorance wasn't really beneficial for their longevity. Meaning, your ancestors were pretty good at spotting the negative, and chances are your brain is as well.

For example: if you've ever had an evaluation from a superior where you get a glorifying review about your performance, yet at the end you get the "items to improve upon" list.... You may have noticed that last bit is the *only* thing your mind wants to think about! Now you know why. It's the jaguar.

Likewise, if we let our mind run wild in a relationship, it's going to filter out everything that our partner has done wrong, everything that irritates us, and everything that was even slightly disrespectful. And then, when the mind has that part in focus, it will start to ruminate and ruminate. As soon as you've crossed eyes with that big black predatory jaguar cat, *all* you'll be able to think about is how to not end up on its dinner plate. It's a life-saving part of our brain that can sadly serve us some dangerous mind games within relationships and other areas of life. This is why and how perpetual worries are born.

Needless to say, hostility, contempt, and resentment thrive on this feature of our minds. As everything we *don't* like about our partner starts to pile up in our field of vision, we may start to nag, become angry, respond in not so kind ways, and complain even more. It's as if we can *only* see the parts we dislike, so we forget to enjoy and cherish all the good. If you suffer from this predicament, rest assured, it is totally natural. Yet, the deadly poisons arsenic and cyanide are all natural as well, so it's not necessarily good for us.

So, how do the happy couples deal with this? Their minds do it too, given that they are humans like the rest of us. Well, they override it by using a zest of emotional intelligence yet again. They will deliberately choose to change focus to everything they *do* like. A little trick one of the couples I had interviewed told me about is to have a little photo album of "happy moments" at hand on our phone or elsewhere. When our ego starts to single out our lover as the cause of bad feelings and wants to increase hostility, we look at those pictures. That will then bring up the positive and loving feelings that are associated with them. This can work really well, as you'll find out in the next chapter.

Why Is He Ignoring Me?

I cannot overemphasize how important the concept from the previous chapter is. The mind tricks us all the time! We can feel anxiety when we're not in any danger whatsoever. We can feel unloved or hurt by our partner when nothing is wrong. Something our partner says or does can feel unloving or like an attack when it isn't. And it is indispensable that we manage this on our own. *Especially* when it comes to our irrational needs where we place the bar too high. At that moment we get to choose between hurting the relationship by being too demanding or hooking up the love-hose to our own love ponds.

Let's look at Kathy. Kathy is a great and kind woman, and she's in love with Burt. Burt is a lawyer who's busy working on his career most of the time. He's a nest-builder, and he's looking for financial security. Kathy has emotional empathy and physical closeness as her main love ponds and today, on a beautiful Monday, she feels lonely. Even though they are living together, she hasn't seen much of Burt this past weekend because he was helping out at his parents' house. So at 11 AM she reaches for her phone and calls Burt at work. Burt doesn't pick up. No harm done, for now, but this isn't helping with her loneliness. At 2 PM she wonders why Burt didn't call back during his lunch break. "He must have seen I've called him. Why is he ignoring me? Is something wrong?" she ponders. She picks up her phone and tries again. No answer. Now she starts to feel angry. Her mind has seen the jaguar eyes, and she cannot let this go. Her concentration plummets, and she has a hard time keeping her mind focused on her work. She starts to simulate the criticisms she will unleash on Burt tonight. How dare he! He should know better by now!

Let's teleport to Burt. Burt is a good guy; he knows Kathy wants a lot of attention. They have had this discussion in the early days of their relationship. Kathy would call him at work; Burt would be busy and think, "I'll talk to her tonight." At first, he didn't get that Kathy had an anxious attachment style and just needed to know the connection between them was still fine. A quick sign of life would have been sufficient.

One night, when Kathy took the time to kindly explain this to him, he said, "OK, honey. I'll try to pick up the phone more often," which is what he did from then on. He loved Kathy dearly; it was not a big deal. By picking up the phone or reaching back out to her, she called and contacted him much less because she felt safer and more connected in general. This was logical, given that her love ponds were now filled. But today Burt was at war! The opposing counsel had played a nasty game in one of the cases he was working, and it was all hands on deck. He saw the missed calls but didn't have the time on this feisty Monday to return them.

Kathy now has a very important choice to make. Her mind is starting up the game playing. Her emotional empathy and physical closeness ponds are depleting rapidly. She feels misunderstood and doesn't get why Burt would hurt her feelings so much by *deliberately* ignoring her. She knows his phone is practically glued to his body, so he *has* seen the missed calls. If she lets the mind games play on, they will have a huge fight tonight, and she will greatly harm their bond. Burt will probably withdraw as well, especially given that he will have had a tough day himself, which will make her feel alone even more. Her mind, however, is unaware of all of this. It doesn't care because it's not thinking long term; it's still focusing on the jaguar's eyes. All else has faded away. It's difficult to think clearly because her emotions are trying to take over the steering wheel.

117

Now to you and me it's quite logical that her request for Burt to be on call at all times is completely ridiculous. Yet this is just an example. Our minds may have come up with requests just as unreasonable. I know mine has. That's again because the ego only has one song on its playlist. It's called, "me me me myself and I." The mind tricks us in many ways and will come up with feelings and thoughts that have no validity in the real world. Burt is not behaving like an asshole here, and yet her mind starts to become convinced he is one. Kathy is now officially high maintenance if she continues down this path. And, perhaps most importantly, she's now emptying her own love ponds... *all by herself!* The more she continues down this path, the more unloved she'll feel.

So what can she do?

Should she assertively tell Burt he should always be available to her, whatever is going on at work? Shouldn't relationships be about communication? About openly stating what we feel? Shouldn't this then include *all* requests including the unreasonable ones?

No, because again, there is no room for doormats in any great relationship. We can't request for our partner to become one either.

There's only one solution. Kathy needs to become aware of the jaguar; she needs to understand that her mind is fearful now and feels a fear of death. I'm not exaggerating. As childish as this may seem, for someone who's anxiously attached, the potential loss of attachment will generate a fear that's as high as the actual fear of death. I don't know what it will be for you, but there will be behaviors that, when your partner executes them, will make you lose your balance quickly.

Kathy is a woman I have personally coached in the past, and I had trained her to look at a loving picture of Burt at moments like these to create the much-needed pattern interrupt and to take her mind off of the jaguar, if only for a couple of seconds.

Then I asked her to self-regulate her love pond. This is a very powerful strategy, as you're about to see.

With her blinders now lifted thanks to the loving picture of Burt, Kathy started to ask herself a couple of important questions that would help her eventually calm down and feel safe and loved again—*without* any of Burt's input. The questions were: "I'm focusing on the jaguar's eyes here, where are the butterflies? Is there anything positive? Can I find proof of him giving me what I need? Of him choosing to give me what I need?"

Yes, she could. "Last week when I felt lonely and reached out, he got back to me within the hour. I can indeed find plenty of examples that prove what's happening now is the exception, not the rule. Burt is probably just busy."

And there it was; that very last sentence set her free. Burt was probably not a big asshole after all. She wouldn't need to change the locks or take out the whip to teach him a lesson. Her mind had now dismissed the jaguar's eyes. Kathy started to calm down and could again focus on her to-do list at work.

When Burt got home that night, an hour later than usual, Kathy had made them dinner and told him in a friendly way, "Here, babe. You must have had a busy day at work, let's eat and relax." This could have played out very differently, to the amusement of their goldfish. Burt had honestly expected Kathy to be a bit mad, but to his surprise, she wasn't. Now *he* felt safer as well, and they spent a relaxing night together. Kathy had singlehandedly strengthened their relationship on a day that old Kathy might have smashed it to pieces.

If you are not anxiously attached, Kathy's fears will seem strange, possibly childish or weak. Nevertheless, we do not choose our triggers and most of our needs. Some are deeply rooted into our subconscious brain. All we can do then is learn how to deal with them as best as we can when they arise. That's what Kathy did.

Where are your weak points? Are there areas where you may be too demanding or where love ponds may be *too* sensitive? Where could you use this technique? If you look back at your current or past relationships, did you ever lose it when you really shouldn't have? When your partner didn't do anything wrong but your mind was convinced he or she did? Or did you ever feel very unloved by your partner when there was no reason to (looking back at it)? *That's* when you should apply this technique the next time. Because chances are it will happen again.

This technique to self-regulate a love pond is powerful and works in two ways:

- Find proof of recent events that filled your most important love ponds. In Kathy's example, she looks for moments of physical closeness and emotional empathy. Recalling those moments will help resurface the accompanying good emotions.
- Focus on the other love ponds. What other loving actions has your partner performed? This will not help as much as the first step. However, all the love ponds have some importance, so it will help soothe you.

This works like magic when you feel neediness, loneliness, anger, or resentment building up in yourself with no valid reason.

What's appearing here is never meant to dismiss actual bad behavior! We're not looking for excuses when someone deliberately hurt us. It's instead for the moments when you'll feel unloved and there really is no reason to or when your partner is preoccupied, has his or her own demons to tackle, and is less tuned in to what you need to feel loved and happy. Our partners are living beings with things on their own minds, after all. They are not our servants. Sometimes we don't see what's right in front of us because our mind is very busy making a mountain out of a molehill elsewhere. This is one of the many reasons why all the successful couples I've studied were diligently applying emotional intelligence to their relationships. *They had to.* And when this willingness comes from both sides, the relationship can truly flourish and thrive.

"But No I Didn't!"

"But no I didn't..." is one of the great relationship destroyers that empties out multiple love ponds at once, with the empathy one going first. It will come as no surprise that kindness and love are friends while nastiness, hostility, and *even defensiveness* won't really nurture love at all.

Jack and Jill were eating out at a restaurant, and I happened to be waiting for a friend at the table next to them. It was a beautiful and warm summer night in Paris. We were sitting almost all alone and given that they spoke English and heard me speak French to the waiter, they spoke openly and didn't hush their voices. Here was part of their conversation:

Jill: "So I was thinking about my idea to start giving seminars. I'm picturing a great location, somewhere close to the beach. I could invite a lot of women, and we could all have fun!"
Jack: "Ah ha-ha, yeah, the seminars. And what will the seminar be about then?"
Jill: "Why are you making fun of my idea?"
Jack: "I'm not making fun of your idea! I didn't do that!"
Jill: "Yes you did. You just laughed!"
Jack: "What? I didn't laugh! At all! I'm sure I didn't laugh. Why would you say that? Are you trying to ruin our evening?"

Since I was looking forward to an evening free of relationship trouble, I looked over right away and said, "Do you guys love each other?"

That was enough of a pattern interrupt, given that it was not in the French language they had expected me to speak. No need to bring out the goldfish here.

"What?" Jack said, a bit startled. I couldn't blame him, but I nonetheless repeated the question.

"That's none of your business," Jack replied. It wasn't indeed.

"I'm not sure anymore," Jill stepped in. "I'm not sure he loves me."

"What?" a startled Jack said again, turning back to Jill. He was probably as surprised by her opening up to a total stranger as he was by her actual answer. "Why would you say that? Why else am I here, on the other side of the world, in Paris, the city of what? Of LOVE! With you!"

Jack was a feisty one. Unbeknownst to himself, Jack was making the same mistake twice and singlehandedly started to dismantle the important bond between them. Jack's mind was focusing on the jaguar's eyes. His girlfriend's reaction had triggered him hard.

"Jack," I said. "I know and understand it's really inappropriate for me to eavesdrop, and rest assured, I wouldn't like it at all if it were happening to me. But I did overhear your conversation. I help people with relationship problems, and I just want you both to become aware of what's going on here. Because I sense that you may not see it at the moment."

Jill was curious to find out what it was. Jack, not so much. Understandably, considering Jack clearly was the victim here. The poor man wasn't doing anything wrong at all. He was the peaceful angel under attack by his out-of-her-mind devilish girlfriend Jill and now by the rude trilingual stranger sitting next to them... poor Jack.

As I slowly sipped from my glass of French bubbles, I started to explain, "You both are talking at different frequencies right now, and what you're saying is not arriving at the other side of the table. I'm sure you both love each other, but you *both* are creating the fight that is taking place here. And it's done in such an interesting way that you may be surprised at how it works. You're both stuck in a mind game. Jack, you did laugh at Jill when she talked about the seminar—"

"But no I—" Jack began.

"Jack, you really did. I heard it, and that's totally fine because you weren't making fun of Jill."

"No! I wasn't."

"But she thought so. She felt hurt. And that could have been uncalled for, but she still felt hurt. At that moment, she feels rejected and sees the safety and the connection of the relationship melt away. Our emotions are wrong more often than not, but even when they are wrong, they are present. We need to deal with them. So as Jill is feeling hurt and attacked by the man she loves, what does that man do? He takes out his protective shields, creates more distance, climbs high on his high horse, and while looking down upon Jill, says, 'No, your perception of what just happened is totally wrong. I am right. I am the all-knowing oracle' as you are swinging around with your sharp blade, ready to hurt her some more. Is that the type of knight in shining armor you want to be, Jack?"

Jack started to laugh now, at himself, and surprised me in doing so. I was sure he would have become more defensive, but he didn't. He saw his wrongdoing. When his girlfriend feels hurt, she feels hurt. And that's that. Whether it was uncalled for doesn't matter. If he wants to be loving, he cannot judge, but he cannot defend either. She's not the enemy. She never is! She's hurt, and even though that will very often not make any sense whatsoever to him, he needs to acknowledge it.

"So what should I have done then?" Jack asked.

"You could have said, 'Oh, did I laugh? I'm sorry. I'm not making fun of you. If it seems that I'm unsupportive, then know that I am supportive.'"

It's as simple as that. We don't crawl onto our high horse; we acknowledge the feeling and do not defend or attack.

Being defensive may sound inconsequential, but it *is* a very big deal. It's still a sign of hostility. We only defend against the enemy. In Jack and Jill's case, these are cracks in their bond that would lead to Jill not sharing or being hesitant to share since she fears Jack's reaction. And whenever fear enters a relationship, it's headed toward the exit.

But defensiveness is also important to Jack because had he continued down that road, he would have thought Jill was crazy, high maintenance, ungrateful for their vacation, and deliberately making it hard on him. Poor Jack indeed.

Jill was simply a hurt woman in need of love and support from her man. Jack proved to be just as sensitive, as demonstrated by his own angry reaction. The reason why Jill was so sensitive that night, as I found out later, was that both her brother and father always ridiculed her when she was growing up. Whatever idea she had, they made fun of it and told her it would fail. And because Jack seemed to take the same approach (even when he wasn't), her subconscious brain got triggered, alarms were ringing, and she could only focus on the hidden jaguar. They both had the respect love pond as a very sensitive one and were *both* evacuating love water by the bucket in each other's pond, instead of restoring the peace.

Here too, the rule of thumb is: instead of tackling each other, we should tackle the problem. The more we are willing to understand the reasons for our partner's reactions instead of defending against them, the better the relationship will be.

Discovering Your and Your Partner's Love Ponds

Now that we've dived into some major relationship destroyers, let's go over how to focus on each other's love ponds so you both can pour love into the right love ponds and feel like you're on top of the world.

Even though I've given plenty of examples of how to fill the different love ponds when I was describing them, know that what fills them will differ from one person to the next. That's why it will be very important to listen to the requests and the very specific needs your partner has. That's the best way to hit the bull's-eye and hit your lover with a potent love potion.

As you've undoubtedly discovered, this entire book is about needs. The scientist Helen Fisher wrote about the hierarchy of needs and famous psychologist Abraham Maslow came up with his own hierarchy of needs. We're all driven by needs that we perpetually try to fill. Relationships are special because our **dominant** need is to have our partner at least partially look out for our unique set of *other* needs. The clearer the picture of the needs in the relationship, the better and more loved both people in it will feel. Although our needs can be as varied as the weather, they all belong to the same set of categories, which I've called the love ponds.

Let me first stress why this chapter is *so* important. It's become pretty evident throughout the book that when you fill your lover's ponds, you'll get great behavior in return. However, we need to monitor our *own* love ponds as well. They are the ones that make *us* unhappy, grumpy, and negative.

A couple of weeks ago, I noticed I was snapping at my girlfriend. I wasn't really friendly, and I had a short fuse combined with a bad temper a few days in a row. I was becoming my worst self. The old me wouldn't even have become aware of it, given that I had a lot going on in my life at that time. This time, however, I turned inward and asked myself: "What's going on? Is there a love pond in trouble?" There was! I had aching unfulfilled needs that I was unaware of. My girlfriend and I had been so busy in our own lives that it had been a long time since we went for a long walk together or had taken the time to just sit and be together. My physical closeness and emotional empathy ponds—both not very important love ponds in my personal case—were running on empty, and I hadn't noticed until now.

As you can see, even the least important ponds eventually matter, they may even be the sneakiest ones given that you may not be aware of right away. So I communicated this to my girlfriend and we planned to spend some quality time together. As soon as we did, I felt better and noticed that I effortlessly became more loving toward her again.

Finding the importance and love level of the ponds is not always an easy endeavor. You may, at first, not even know your own most important love ponds, let alone their status. Nevertheless, I've found that successful couples are really attentive when it comes to this. We're continuously communicating the status of our love ponds to one another. The question is: Is anyone listening?

Jack from the previous chapter will probably have had past experiences with Jill's reaction to his laughs or with the way he responds to her ideas. Based on that single interaction I overheard, I knew that the respect love pond and the empathy pond were really high up on her list, which Jill later confirmed. Jack's reaction, on the other hand, proves respect was equally important to him as well. He was very sensitive in that area. All of the couples we've seen throughout this book could have avoided a lot of heartache had they been paying more attention to the status of their lover's *and their own* love ponds. We just need to listen.

Suppose a woman, Leah, says, "Mike, I really need you to help out more around the house." If Mike isn't listening (or doesn't want to), he may say to himself, "I believe I do enough. I work hard every day and help pay the bills." Or (and this is an interesting one) good old Mike may think, "Yeah, she really does a lot around the house. I'll surprise her with flowers and a vacation!"

Good old Mike. The flowers may make her day, but this is only temporary relief since he still didn't pay attention to her need. He didn't listen. Instead, he filled up the wrong love pond. Love is a choice, as is choosing to listen and pay attention. A better answer would have been, "Sure, honey. How can I help? What do you need help with?" and then do it.

The challenge doesn't just lie with Mike, in this case. Leah, the woman in our example here, must use the right form of communication as well. It can't be hostile. Imagine if she had said, "Mike, why don't you ever help out around the house?" That would have made it a lot more difficult for Mike to respond positively. It's not that we need to sugarcoat our messages, but we must communicate with an open and loving heart and without resentment, contempt, or criticism as an undertone. Nagging and negativity never work. We have to be the bigger person first if we want the same treatment in return... *even* when we're frustrated because it's not the first time we've asked it. Always keep the end goal in mind.

Now let's generalize a bit. When you're looking for your partner's most important love ponds, gender may play a role. Respect, as I've learned through my interviews and practical experience, is often a *very sensitive* love pond for men. Respect, of course, matters a lot to both sexes. All ponds matter to some extent. Men, however, have more fragile egos. Their respect pond dries out quickly and will need care. (These are generalizations and there are exceptions, but I found this to be true.) You can compare the fragility of most men's egos to a house of cards about ten stories high. It only takes a sneeze to take it all down. When you respect a man, on the other hand, he will feel like a king, and it will bring out his best behavior. All the men that will strongly disagree with these statements have just proven my point.

Showing respect to a man is really easy. Make him feel like a man. Give him a compliment on his manliness here and there. Tell him why you respect him (and get ready to be specific). Compliment how he protects you, how he makes you feel safe, how you're proud of him working hard, how much he has achieved, and so on. And above all, never ever publicly criticize him. Criticism is bad for relationships at any time, but when you use it on a man while he's amongst friends or other people, it's a nuclear torpedo. Of course, men shouldn't critique women in public or anywhere else either; that goes without saying.

Emotional empathy, on the other hand, even though it matters to both genders, will be on the top of the list for a lot of women, given that they are more emotional by design, as proven by plenty of scientific research.[7] In general, a lot of women love to be able to talk about and share feelings *much*

---

[7] Journal of Neuroscience, 2015 Jan 14; 35(2): 599–609. Topologically Dissociable Patterns of Development of the Human Cerebral Cortex https://www.ncbi.nlm.nih.gov/pmc/articles/PMC4293413/

more than men do. They seek a connection with their lover and often do so on an emotional level. When they hit the male stone-cold wall of nothingness, sense his withdrawal, or just get a to-do list of solutions, they often feel unloved and misunderstood. Not to say that there aren't emotional men out there who want to open up and talk about feelings for hours on end, but I'm making very basic generalizations here based on my own research and experience.

What men can do is step in that emotional circle and apply the aforementioned techniques involving emotional empathy. Don't minimize feelings. Don't try to solve them. Instead, acknowledge them without judgment. Make the connection. A lot of women are simply trying to get the signal through to the man they are with.

Regardless, now that I'm generalizing anyway, I've very often seen these two (respect and emotional empathy) together with the fun love pond at the top of the list for both genders when it comes to their sensitivity. These ponds empty rapidly. If you don't know where to begin, start with these three ponds and make sure they are nicely filled for the both of you.

Ask yourself these questions:
- Is what I'm doing respectful or inconsiderate?
- Is my behavior loving or *un*loving?
- Am I stepping into their emotional circle without judging?
- Am I communicating in a negative way?
- Is there fun in our relationship, *even* when life gets hard?

These will be important questions. Nevertheless, we're not just looking for the status of the most important and obvious love ponds. As we've seen, they all matter. When a not so important pond is drying up, you'll still get weird and possibly unexplainable behavior from your partner, like when I was snapping at my girlfriend for no reason. If yours are drying up, you'll still feel unloved. So we need to listen, continuously, for signs that a certain pond requires our attention. And remember, the importance and fragility of love ponds change throughout our life stages. We have to keep our finger on the pulse.

Here are some specific steps to figure out the more important love ponds and their status, so you can become aware of those running on empty.

Ask

I know, I have my Captain Obvious hat on again. One of the ways to decipher the importance of certain love ponds *and* how to fill them is to just ask our partner what it is they need to feel loved. We should always do this, given that someone's needs to feel loved can be *really* specific (and can change). As you've seen, there are many ways to fill up the love ponds and that too will be very personal. Someone with physical closeness as the most important love pond may for instance surprisingly not be a fan of hand-holding and cuddling. Yet they may feel really loved when their partner checks in with them often during family get-togethers or when out with friends. Take the time to discuss the specificities, and don't be afraid to make actual lists of what's important to feel loved.

That said, we're not always consciously aware of those specific needs. The answers we get may not always represent the truth either. Our partner may be afraid to own up to the truth, or they may just not know.

Hence, we will oftentimes have to do our homework and investigate our lover's behavior. Here are some ways to dig deeper.

Look for Criticisms

Criticisms and complaints are usually unmet needs in disguise. They are frequently simple cries for love. What are the "you nevers," "why don't you evers," and "you used tos" that keep coming back? These are telltale signs of your or your partner's unmet needs and emptied love ponds.

These are tough because chances are it's not the first time the request has been made (that's why it escalated to the criticism level), and it will be hard to comply given that criticisms always hurt our feelings. But we both have to. If we don't bother to listen or fulfill our partner's important, reasonable needs, then there really is no relationship.

If we put our best foot forward and we're not treated well, then we know we're in a relationship with the wrong partner. But in many cases, simple requests only rise to the criticism level because nobody was listening when they were said lovingly at first.

Look for Eyes that Light Up

Someone whose love pond is getting filled up can't help but feel like birds do when spring comes. They will be more energized, playful, and loving toward you. Look for the things you did that made your partner open up, become emotional (positively), or otherwise happy. When you see any or all of these signs, you're doing it right and are focusing on the right love ponds. If a woman, for instance, wants to know how important respect is to her guy, I will ask her to tell him in passing: "I really respect you," and then change the subject or leave. The "Really? Why?" will follow more often than not. And then, once she has given him the reasons, she will probably be surprised of the *unusually* kind behavior that will follow. Chances are his eyes will have lit up *so* much that astronauts could see him from space.

If you're figuring out your own love ponds, then a good question to ask yourself is: "What do I absolutely love that my partner does? When was the last time that I felt really loved? What makes me feel on top of the world?" That will point you in the direction of your most important love ponds and the specific needs related to them. Make sure they are filled up regularly, and don't be afraid to ask for it! Our partners are not clairvoyants; they may be unaware or have seemingly more important things on their plate given that they are human beings with plenty of urgencies in their own lives.

Look at the Opposites

Another great way to find out the importance of the love ponds is to focus on what empties them. Is there anything that, if you or your lover is not getting it, makes you feel alone or ignored? What makes you or your lover angry, disappointed, or withdrawn almost instantly? What makes you feel hurt and lash out? Where are those landmines usually situated?

These are the so-called pain points, and we saw plenty of those during the couples' examples you got throughout this book. When pressed, they hurt, and an explosion of anger or a full withdrawal may follow. These pain points are more often than not directly linked to the most crucial and sensitive love ponds.

What makes your lover or you feel alone or ignored, even though you are together? What makes you feel like the bond has been broken? What generates anxiety or anger? Those are very important signals that some people repeatedly keep missing.

And remember, we may think certain reactions from our lover or even ourselves are foolish, childish, too sensitive, and so on. We may want to sweep them under the rug, but they happen! We must deal with them if we want a thriving relationship.

Look at Requests

Another method to determine suffering love ponds is by listening closely to requests. Those also unveil the unmet needs. Thankfully, it doesn't always have to end up in anger. If I tell my girlfriend that I really don't want to be the only one maintaining the garden, then I'm communicating that I need more help with the nest-building. That pond is suffering. If I say, "Are you going away with your girlfriends again? We don't see each other very often, do we?" or "When we are out with friends, you're almost never standing by my side; it's like I don't exist" then I'm communicating physical closeness is important and that my love pond is running on empty.

I'll give you some often-used requests per love pond. Each and every one of these sentences can point to a lack of love in the corresponding pond.

Here are some of the telltale signs your partner may give:

Respect
I feel like I don't matter to you.
Am I still important to you?

I don't like it when you talk to me like *that*.
You should have told me.
Please stop asking me to change who I am.
Why didn't you ask for my opinion?
It feels like it's always your way or the high way.
Do you still love/like me?
Do you appreciate me?
It's as if I'm not even here....
Does my opinion matter to you?
What do you like about me?
Last night, when you suddenly left with your friends, you left me all alone at home and you didn't even consult with me. That doesn't feel good.
You told me you would call, but then you didn't. That hurts.

Fun
I want to do something fun with you.
I miss the time when we used to....
Remember when we _____; we don't do that anymore.
I don't want to fight.
We're fighting so much.
It's like all we do is talk about what needs to get done.
Please don't yell at me.
Please don't raise your voice.
I don't want to feel this way.
Why don't we _____ next weekend?
John and Sara went hiking last week; why don't we do that next weekend?

Emotional Empathy
I miss how we used to have time to talk when we...
Thanks, but you don't need to tell me what to do, I just wanted to share what happened.
It feels like you're not there for me.

All you do is work/hang out with friends/work out...
(meaning I miss the connection we used to have)
I feel lonely, even though we live together.
I miss our conversations.
I miss just talking to you.
I miss you. (Even though you see each other often or live together.)

Nest-Building

I know you don't like it when I work so much, but it's really important to me. (This usually follows remarks about working too hard that are starting to hinder the nest-building.)
I feel like I'm the only one who cares for our house/garden/...
I could really use a hand with...
Could you help out some more with....
You promised that you would help out with... (but you didn't)
I don't like it when plans change.
You promise? Will you not forget this time?
Let's stick to the plan please.
But you promised?
Let's save money for....

Physical Closeness

When was the last time we just spent time together, without feeling rushed, without having anything else to do?
Why are you walking so far away from me?
I don't want to go alone.
Don't you think I'm attractive any longer?
I miss you. (Especially when this is used even though you're living together. This here can indeed both point to a lack of emotional empathy and physical closeness.)
I wish you would have been there.
Why don't you come with me when I _____ next weekend?

When we're out with friends or family, you seem to distance yourself from me...
Come sit next to me.
I'd like you to watch this movie with me.
Care to join me?

I Thought of You
This is a trickier one request-wise given that few requests will be made here. You'll notice disappointment, however, when you forgot something or when you didn't foresee something that was easy to foresee had you "thought" of your lover.

Mothering
I've got so much on my mind; I don't know what to think about first.
Would you mind taking care of that? (Related to organizing something, not an actual task.)
I could really use your advice; how would you do this? (Ah, one of the exceptions where we can actually give solutions.)
I feel like I have to think of *everything*....
Can you help pick out a gift for my parents?
I'll go shop for the groceries, but what should I buy?
When do we need to leave tonight?
What kind of clothes should I bring?
Would you mind dealing with this insurance claim?

As you can feel, these are questions from someone who is in need of some assistance with the organization of everything.

Conclusion

These requests will point you in the right direction. Needless to say, all of this is about unfulfilled needs. I've just grouped them in 7 different love ponds to see the wood for the trees, but the needs are what counts. They will always surface throughout the requests, frustrations, and discussions you'll have with your partner. If you can't figure out the love pond, go for the actual need and try to fulfill the request. If you *can* figure out the love pond *behind* the need, then you have more options aside from the direct request and can use the ideas I've given while describing the various love ponds. Feel free to test and play with it and look for those eyes that light up. They always will when you've hit the bull's-eye.

And remember, if you're the one making the requests, try to be very specific. Most of the requests I've just given are not specific, that's why they keep you guessing and are not blatantly obvious. If, for instance, emotional empathy and physical closeness are two of your more important love ponds that need a refill, be specific and say: "Honey, I feel like I've lost the connection with you. I know we spend a lot of time together, but I need a real connection. Why don't we go to a national park for a long walk next weekend? We can sit on that bench we used to sit on while we were dating and have a good talk. I want to be able to sit next to you and talk to you and not be busy cooking or watching TV at the same time." That's specific. If you believe life and your relationship became boring and your fun pond is aching, don't say: "We should do something fun together," Instead, suggest something specific: "I know how we both said we wanted to learn horseback riding. I see the club has an opening next weekend. Want to go?"

The less cryptic we are, the faster our lover can fulfill our needs. Because if we have given them what they need, they will be eager to love us in return.

Repairing the *Really* Broken Relationship

This chapter only applies to you if you sense you're in a relationship that's really close to the exit. If that isn't where you're at, feel free to skip it.

Our brain and our entire behavior are designed to avoid pain and gain pleasure. If you rock climb for the first time in your life and break an ankle, chances are this will be the last time you'll go vertical on rock formations. If you hang out with a new friend one night and have the best time ever, chances are you'll do it again. It's a simple yet powerful concept that drives a lot of human behavior.

As you fell in love with your partner and exchanged that very first kiss, you were both filled with the hormones and neurotransmitters of pure exhilarating happiness like dopamine, oxytocin and certain opioids, as we've seen. There is no better feeling on earth to most of us. Needless to say, you wanted more! "Let's see each other again (and again)," you promised. And you did! And you had so much fun. You felt like your deepest needs were fulfilled, as if the future would bring nothing but mellow happiness. Since the other person was always present when you felt ecstatic, you realized all too well that this person was to be held close—forever, if at all possible.

However, as we've seen, for *some* couples, it's a short-lived period. Negativity and irritation start to trickle in. They are unaware of this and might fail to do anything to fix it. Worse, they probably keep adding negativity and gladly sprinkle *more* criticism, resentment, cynicism, and hope that this will, in some miraculous way, fix everything. It won't. **And then, and this is a turning point in every relationship, comes the moment where for the very first time ever, their lover**

makes them more *un*happy than happy. This starts to create conflicts in their brain. A part of them wants to be with their lover, to get the pleasure that person used to bring, but another part believes the relationship is starting to hurt too much and that they'll need to withdraw to avoid the pain.

This is an interesting and a pivotal moment. This is when men start to live in their garage or man cave. They come home from work later and later, even though their to-do list may have been completed hours earlier. Women start to avoid the mutual home (or seeing their man) as well; they sign up for book clubs, yoga classes, cooking classes, or take super long nature walks. And here's the kicker: they're not really doing it for their health, out of interest, or to have social bonds with others. (These would all be good reasons, of course.) They're avoiding home because home is where it hurts.

When a relationship starts to experience plenty of negative moments and the joyful intimate bits start to be lacking, there *is* no relationship any longer. My own father virtually lived in the garage in the last ten years of the marriage with my mother. He purposely came home late from work after we had already eaten dinner. Then he hid in the garage on the weekends, fiddling with tools and working in the garden. He gladly went for the groceries and would take any excuse he could to get out of the house. Why wouldn't he? Indoors was where the blaming and the yelling was.

As soon as there is a negative atmosphere between two people, they will start to grow apart. If you're meeting a friend and all she does is complain and talk about subjects that make you feel bad afterward, how long will you keep meeting up with her? The growing apart is natural then. We are attracted to what makes us feel good and repulsed by what makes us feel down or hurt. And this repulsion is exactly what happened in relationships that drifted toward very rough waters.

So what's the secret to fixing all of this? If and when both parties are still willing to make it work, we'll have to *artificially* recreate the fun from the earlier days. Given that the entire brain and body are looking for pleasure and run away from pain, we'll need to artificially inject some fun back into the relationship.

This seems fake, and it is. *But it won't feel that way!*

Step One

Be as loving as you can and start pouring love in each other's most important or empty love ponds. You'll need to figure out what those love ponds are, and that requires some communication as we've seen. Your partner cannot read your mind. You'll both have to explain, in detail, what it is that makes you feel loved, safe, and connected. Given that the relationship is already in the danger zone, do not guess! Talk about it. One of the most important mistakes I see in relationships is thinking, "I like to receive loving text messages and pictures because that proves that my lover has been thinking of me. So, I'm going to show my love by also sending loads of messages." If the partner is a nest-builder, he will still feel unhappy and unloved. Remember, we are all wired differently and our love ponds will be too.

Be really specific. For example: what my partner needs to feel loved is that I always ask for her permission whenever I'm about to decide something that has an impact on her. (In this case, respect is huge on her list.) If I invite friends over, I ask first. If I'll be late, I let her know as soon as I become aware that I'll be late. Now her second most important pond was emotional empathy, so whenever I come home from work, even though I'd rather run to the TV to sit back and relax, I'll ask her how her day went. I'll listen without judging or offering to fix it. And only when she feels understood and heard will I turn on the TV or go for a jog.... and so on. This can be really specific.

That is step number one. Don't guess. Figure out what each other's most important love ponds are as a team, and start doing what your partner desires *even if it feels artificial*. Both parties then partake in this activity, which may feel very awkward at first, given the current health of the relationship. If you have to go first, that's OK. My experience taught me that if the partner still cares for you, he or she will follow suit before you know it. When your partner feels loved, he or she will open up and become more intimate. But we may need to go first and keep it up for a while. We cannot get our needs met in a relationship if we refuse to satisfy the needs of our partner. I've always presupposed in this book that you're dealing with a good person, someone who's not out to neglect you or hurt you deliberately. If your lover is a good person and clearly wants to work on the relationship as well, then there is no harm in going first.

This is indeed never a quid pro quo. It won't work then. How easy is it to truly enjoy a loving massage, if you know that there's a timer running in the background and after your five minutes are up, you'll need to do the same for your partner? It probably won't be very relaxing. In this exercise, we give whether we get something in return or not (that's not the point of the exercise anyway). All human beings want to be loved without feeling that they have to perform something in return. And it's just because this exercise creates that safe environment, without pressure, that the possibility that you *do* start to get loads of love in return is so great.

143

Conflicts and differences do not need to be resolved! Some couples live happily ever after with the same conflicts and differences they've had since their sixth date. It's the love and the absence of pain and hostility that need work. You can have a loving and respectful conflict or disagreement with your partner that won't harm the relationship. It's contempt and resentment that will destroy it from the inside out. That's what we'll need to wipe off the table.

You may wonder why this artificial step would work. As soon as we start to feel good again *because* of our partner (and vice versa), we'll want to spend more time together and the previous feelings of love and attraction get a chance to resurface. It's that simple. Even when it's artificial in the beginning.

I thought of this strategy while I heard Nobel Prize winner Daniel Kahneman talk about an interesting find in happiness research. Research has proven that when one group of people was asked to put a pencil in their mouth as if they were sucking on a Popsicle, nothing happened. When another group of people was asked to put the pencil in their mouth horizontally, making the two ends exit their lips and thus putting their mouth in the position of a smile, they felt significantly happier.[8] This too was artificial and fake, but the body didn't know the difference and the emotions of happiness followed. That's the same reason why a player is able to make many women fall for him. These women know all too well he's a fake, but they still develop feelings for him. It also explains why some men are known to spend hundreds of dollars per night in a strip club if they've met a stripper who

---

[8] The original study took place in 1988 by Fritz Strack, since then, many others followed.

knows how to give the "girlfriend experience." It can't get more artificial than that, but the body doesn't care.

It's OK to fake it till you make it because we keep the end goal in mind—to have a loving relationship again. And even though there is some pretending involved, we're only doing this exercise because *both* parties in the relationship have decided they want to have a future together. That means there *still is* real love too.

This is an important distinction. One or both of you may need convincing, but only one question matters: "Do you both want to save this relationship?" If the answer is no, then it can all end now. If it is yes, then what's the harm in trying?

When a relationship goes south, one or both parties see the relationship as hurtful or an entrapment. We'll need to turn it around and make both the relationship and the other person a source of pleasure again. Just like it used to be in the earlier days.

Step Two

The second step entails that we cannot behave like enemies but have to act like allies *at all times* during this healing stage. We *completely* cut out negativity. Even though we may feel hurt by the actions or inaction of our partner, we no longer retaliate. Think of the Dr. Goldstein experiment with the wives who had been left by their husbands. We don't fight fire with fire.

For example, if your partner says, "Why don't you ever clean up the kitchen like I do when I cook?" don't defend or retaliate, however hard that is. Instead, act like an ally and say, "You're right. I understand the mess in the kitchen makes you upset." If your partner quips back with another hurtful comment, still do not retaliate. Say simply, "Next time I'll clean it up right away after cooking, even before I serve the food. That way it will be taken care of already." Try fighting fire with love, for a change.

You may feel some resistance as you're reading this, but rest assured, this approach won't turn you into a doormat. Here's what's interesting; this is a very strong, disarming, and friendly approach. Had you defended or attacked, your voices would have been raised even more. However, your partner may now say, "Thanks, I appreciate it. And I'm sorry I'm a bit grumpy tonight. I've had a bad day at work." Part of our brain doesn't like this approach, because it demands to be respected. Well, you won't get any respect by yelling or using a counterattack. The only way to lower the tension is to not rise to their level. Not even once. For as long as it takes, *as long as we're sure our partner means well,* as I presuppose in this particular book. When they don't, there's obviously no reason to stay. You should never be the doormat of someone who *really* has no respect for you. This approach comes from a position of strength. Losing our cool *is* weak behavior; it's exhibit number A of emotional *un*intelligence. I've said it before, but here it goes again: our partner is never the enemy! The moment they become the enemy, there is no relationship anymore. So don't treat them like one.

Second, we leave past behavior in the past! The Goldstein experiment I explained in the respect chapter proved how important that was as well. Had the wife continued to blame her ex-husband for his past behavior, the love between them would not have returned. Let the past go and start fresh; if you cannot, there's no point in moving forward anyway. Here too you'll have to decide if the past represents a deal breaker or not. If it doesn't, let it go, and it will soon get out of viewing distance, just as when you drop something in a pond. As long as you don't keep pulling it back up, it will sink away out of sight.

Love never magically arrives in long-term relationships, especially not when the relationship already is in trouble. We need to work hard for it! And realizing that we play an amazingly important part in this relationship (by choosing to let go of past behavior and to not get angry and retaliate) is what gives us the control we've been looking for.

If we stay calm, friendly, and loving and are *still* treated badly week after week, then at least we know we've given it *all we've got*, and that it's time to confidently end the chapter. We won't have to worry later whether we made the right decision or not, we'll know beyond any doubt. But before we can get there, we need to give it all we've got! In order to be loved, we need to be prepared to give love first.

Try these two steps and please remember that your partner's possible hostility may just be a result of the hurt and disconnection your lover feels toward you. We all act out in different and very emotional ways when we feel rejected.

Chances are, as both of your love ponds are being filled up, as the bond is slowly being restored, you'll feel the love between the both of you grow significantly. Then, from then on, avoid making the same mistake twice. Keep watering the love ponds, and do everything in your power to stay away from the relationship destroyers—anger and hostility.

They Live Happily Ever After or Do They?

Don't you love how every romantic flick ends with the protagonists falling in love and sailing off into the known future of unconditional love and never-ending blissful happiness?

In the real world, we have a better chance of meeting two rhinos passionately playing chess. "For better or for worse" and similar sentences that have been used for centuries in many religions around the world give away a clue that both ridiculously good *and* painfully hard times lie ahead for every couple. Only the couples prepared to both enjoy the sunshine and weather the storms can make it.

The most important ingredient to making it work, if you ask me, is emotional intelligence—choosing what's best for the longevity of the relationship regardless of what our feelings are trying to make us do or say. Emotional intelligence and thus self-control cut through anything. It's the great differentiator between a loving relationship with fully filled love ponds and a relationship that looks like a battlefield.

I hear you. Controlling your emotions is not easy. It just isn't. I myself have been practicing this emotional intelligence play ever since I read Daniel Goleman's book *Emotional Intelligence* many years ago, and I still have work to do. But here's the good news. This is like a muscle. If you've ever been to a gym, you might have noticed that the weights you absolutely cannot pick up become easy to lift if you gradually work your way up to them while letting your muscles evolve and get stronger over time. Emotional intelligence is no different.

Our habits create our mind's many neural pathways. When you were a toddler, walking required a great deal of mental energy. You were not able to do it while dialing a phone number or sipping from a bottle of water. You had to consciously go over all of the motions to take your first actual steps. This gradually grew into a new neural pathway, a habit. Now your brain can do it effortlessly, and you can combine walking with other activities. The same goes for managing our emotions. It takes a lot of practice, but it will become easier and easier until it is eventually an effortless automatism.

So the next time you fall hard for someone or feel an emotional uprise because of your partner, say to yourself, "These are just feelings. It's like an energy going through my body. These feelings do not always reflect reality. What's the best course of action to make this relationship work? To *make* love?" And then do that. I promise you, it will make a tremendous difference.

Consider the relationship the beautiful castle you both live in and protect it with force.

We all mess up and make mistakes. So do our partners. A lot of their bad behavior was not personal at all, even though it *really* felt that way. Just like us, they are fighting internal battles every day. Life gets tough every now and then. But the more we both learn to cut through the fog and feelings that aren't serving us, the more time we can spend on what matters: looking after all of our love ponds, steering clear of negativity as much as we can and enjoying all of the benefits the relationship offers us.

When we do it right and when we both work hard and try to protect that relationship as much as we can, it will give us some of the best feelings known to humankind. There really is no substitute.

We all deserve to get out needs met, but unlike the movies and fairy tales, it is rarely unconditional. We'll have to work hard for it, as is the case for the fulfillment of so many other needs we have. If you want to satisfy your hunger, you have to farm, hunt, *or* go to work and make money in order to buy your food in a store. If you want to feel loved, you have to love other people and care about what's important to them. You'll have to hunt and farm as well. A friendship or a romantic relationship can only thrive when both people make that choice. As we've seen, we all have an ego with "me me me" tattooed on its forehead. But in every kind of relationship, we'll have to train our powers to supersede that.

Even if we have the best relationship in the world, we'll still be frustrated at times. Our partners won't be perfect and will often misunderstand what we really meant. Decisions will be made that clearly did not take our wishes into account; bathrooms and kitchens will be left dirtier than we'd prefer, and, above all, our partner will not read our mind and adapt to our every whim. But when push comes to shove, we wouldn't want it any other way. Because it's all part of love and life. There's only one series of questions that counts: does our partner mean well? Does our lover have a kind and good heart? Does our companion love us? If the answers are "yes," then we struck gold.

I sincerely hope both you and your partner will make the delicate science and art of making love a lifelong hobby. And I wish you good luck on your journey.

Final Words

Thank you for reading this book and making it till the end. I hope you found it inspiring. I've loved writing it for you. I've spent years researching these topics and coaching people to get results and overcome challenges. I hope you'll use what I've described. You deserve the results that go with it!

If you didn't like anything in the book, please reach out to me at brian@briannox.com. I really value your feedback and will take it to heart for the next books I write.

Did you like it? I sincerely hope so. Please share your thoughts on Amazon so other people just like you can find out more about the book. Reviewing is easy. Go to the book by typing the title in Amazon, scroll down to the review section, and click on "Write a customer review." You have my eternal gratitude.

Thanks for reading!

Brian
- Briannox.com

P.S. **And if you want even more tips and strategies**, sign up for my FREE advanced tactics newsletter on scienceofmakinglove.com and join the 94,745 people who already receive it.

Made in the USA
San Bernardino, CA
27 May 2020